BUCK NAKED
An Act of Courage

Written By
Earl Scott

Foreword By
P. Renae Brooks

Copyright © 2016
Earl Scott
All Rights Reserved.
ISBN: 978-0-692-73563-3

Printed in the United States by Morris Publishing®
3212 East Highway 30
Kearney, NE 68847
1-800-650-7888

TABLE OF CONTENTS

Dedication 4

Foreword 7

Preface 9

Introduction 10

Chapter One
    A Little Boy Named Me 16

Chapter Two
    The Beginning of Darkness 22

Chapter Three
    Joining the Circus 50

Chapter Four
    The Road to Damascus 97

Chapter Five
    What About God 113

Chapter Six
    Just Around the Bend 139

Chapter Seven
    The Home Stretch 162

DEDICATION

My sweet mother, Mildred Phipps Scott – for loving me. My father, Earl W. Gibson. My children: La-Shelle Caldwell, Mujahid Amin, Ibaadah Amin and Fareed Amin – all who I dearly love. I express my regrets to my oldest daughter La-Shelle for not being there to see you develop into the great woman you are today.

With this, my first book, I want to express my deep appreciation to others who have enriched my life and helped make me who I am today.

I would like to thank Carolyn Hillsman for helping me to continue more into the light; Dr. Beatrice Berry; Honorable Senator Cory A. Booker; former Mayor of Newark, Sharpe James; Susan Taylor; Honorable Judge Glenn A. Grant; Ruth Williams; Bette Gibson; Rayfield Morton; Ingrid Johnson; Genna Jones; Kareen Motley; Lora Krslich; Eric Ingold; Aunt Mae Stevenson; Dr. Martin Luther King, Jr.; Malcolm X; Ronald Jones (deceased); Michael Jones (deceased); Mildred Lee; Mattie (little mama) Lee; Eve Lewis; the Lewis family of Beech Street; the Allen family; the Simpkins family; the City of Newark; the City of Orange; the religious leaders from all walks of faith; Pastor Keith Wright; Oprah Winfrey for *Super Soul Sunday*; and to the many who have helped shape me as I traveled along the road of life. I want to thank the New Jersey Institute of

Social Justice for petitioning my expungement, clearing and sealing my records which was granted March 1, 2016. I want to thank the Essex County New Jersey Prosecutor Office for their tireless efforts in addressing social justice.

I dedicate this writing to those who have experienced pain, shame, and guilt; who were able, like me, to write a different eulogy about living from day-to-day. To those who are still suffering, I pray they find their way. To my mother who never knew; and to those who loved me and paved a way for me to regain my sanity; to my children who I love dearly; to individuals who have massaged my heart and soul when my tears poured into lakes of forgiveness. To those I may have wronged, I besiege forgiveness for any crime I may have committed in their lives. To my late deceased wife Nur Amin aka as Shirley Jones Davis, who helped to put me on the map; someone who sponged the scars I carried and built a backbone for me to stand erect. I ask forgiveness additionally for leaving her to seek out my destiny. I recognize with love and kindness to Stacie B. Hillsman who scorched me and imprinted my nature and taught me a lesson I needed to learn; never to betray myself as I did. Most of all, thanks to God for forgiving and giving me an opportunity to discover His glory. He had never forgotten me; it was I who had forsaken him. I also pledge this writing to the many that died in Orange, New Jersey and every corner of the earth as a result of addiction and other violent actions as a result of pain. I also devote this book to the people of the Township of Orange, New Jersey – those who knew me, those I never met, and those I may have harmed, and those who I ask to forgive me. I am absolved in His mercy. I praise!

I would be remiss not to mention Lady Sakinah Sylvia Barnett; someone from my days of darkness who always tried to shed a little light on me. Even though she was in my presence, she was protective of me when I came to her house. This woman of thoughtfulness would always look at me in a way of saying *'you do not belong here.'* She would suggest with a motherly concern, *'this isn't a life for you.'* She was strong on me and would let those older characters I was around watch out for me. I want to thank her for loving me and that she will always be a part of who I am today. She was that spirit whispering to do the right thing and her eyes always was demanding she cared.

FOREWORD

The first impression after reading *Buck Naked: An Act of Courage* left me feeling as though I had just completed a life-time of unsolicited advice from a self-help guide – a serious prescription for self-inflicted introspection. We sometimes live our lives through the maze and mayhem we chose to create; but far and few are the souls who will admit their responsibilities of self-inflicted destruction and potential demise. Nonetheless, this book, *Buck Naked: An Act of Courage* is down-right raw, and unequivocally a healing mechanism for anyone who is searching to become.

Each segment of the author's life is brilliantly written. He exposes himself, naked – completely uninhibited to what the world may or may not understand about his journey. Bravo! Mr. Scott – for having the courage to listen to your inner spirit – for using your dimming light as your guidepost to help you through your recovery and ultimately your conquest. Words are oftentimes misunderstood whether written or expressed. I would venture to say that it is not an easy task to pen honest and forthright misgivings of one's life. This book, would absolutely be a vital instrument particularly for the masses who have demonized and plagued themselves in the darkened world of drugs, crime, abandonment, and especially for those who really want to learn how love really does conquer all.

From a spiritual perspective, my heart smiled many times during my read. Why? Because I knew eventually Earl Scott could and would find the solace he longed for – right inside of his being – deep down in the center of existence he found not just a man – he discovered his spirituality – he embraced himself strong enough to allow the negativity to dissolve – he surrounded every emotion with pure honesty – which ultimately led him to himself. He discovered a Supreme Being. He discovered Earl Scott. Thank you for sharing your bravery, courage, insight and inspiration; but most importantly for…

Engaging **A**rticulate **R**eal **L**ove…

Respectfully,
P. Renae Brooks

PREFACE

Dear Mother,
I wanted to let you know what happened to me when you weren't looking. When you weren't looking those who you thought cared about us, never did because they ripped my heart apart. All those times that you were made to believe something was wrong with me; it was because you weren't looking. The times I made you cry was all because you weren't  *looking. The moments you thought I was going to die, I wanted to, because you weren't looking. All the years I worried you, was because you weren't looking. When I was locked away insane, I cried because you weren't looking. I could not tell you of what was being done because they kept you not looking. I am sorry for the harm I did to you, believing you should have been looking. I have forgiven myself as well for thinking you should have been looking. I could not love because my pain made you think it was something different. I can love now and I forgive you even though you weren't looking. As the years have come and whisked by, and many ask me how you come to feel about the world as you do today, I say, I am the son of an illustrious woman who now watches over me.*

INTRODUCTION

According to the English Greek Dictionary the word courage can mean "the virtue that enables us to conquer fear, danger, or adversity." No matter what the context happens to be (physical or moral), courage includes the notion of taking responsibility for decisions and actions. Additionally, the idea involves the ability to perform critical self-assessment, to confront new ideas, and to change.

If you have elected to purchase and read this book, you will experience curiosity, sincerity and openness that will allow you to get to know someone who appreciates the process of healing. Healing from things which touch us all at times – if we are not in denial, healing from an unsettled flow of pain which at times leaves us wounded. I needed to find a way to heal my spirit in order for the rest of me to be renewed and forgiven. I found that process which allowed me to forgive myself to embrace and recapture my soul which I expelled because of trauma and pain.

I looked within myself to capture the significance of constructing my life story through scripting and further identifying the need to constantly replenish. I wanted to share my reconciliation with an audience who would be open to view my life for what it was, and how it turned out to be. I wanted to attract a reader who may find within, a need to forgive themselves or others who may have wronged them. I wanted to present other than typical echoes of literature from the darkness, or another story of ordinariness that our society is so accustomed to reading. I wanted to make emphasis through my own misgivings, the damage I left unattended for so many years as a result of being spiritually dead. I did not want to illustrate or glorify self-destructive behavior with no remedy; but to exemplify how deserting one can have impairment which can transcend and affect ourselves and others' lives. My journey through the maze of life at this point in time has been one of redemption and securing a peace within. I have practiced and come accustomed to not personalizing life's events or to stay outside of the moment. Being in the now takes repetition and preparation.

All stories have a beginning and mine starts with the little boy named me, whose innocence, for no reason other than, was draped and fitted in a suit of pain. A suit that fit too tight and became the foundation for the crimes I committed to myself and others. Removing the suit has been one of forgiveness. How do we begin to stop picking the scabs of our pain? How do we stop removing the stitches of our sufferings and most of all, how do we keep the staples in place for our healing? There is always difficulty in life and people become shattered by many things. This testament of my life is a vehicle to answer these questions by giving meaning, hope, and alternatives to not remaining in any painful circumstances. There are ways to heal and everyone is ensued with the tools to reconcile, restore, and mend their lives. The spirit is the first repair, it is the part of us that needs to be settled and the rest is learning to have faith. *Buck Naked* is a book to help heal, rid the victimization ideology, and refurbish that part of people's lives which makes individuals feel forgiven. It is a reflection on our constant struggle to find the light. It is a mirror that gives insight on how comfortable we become in darkness.

Over 20 plus years ago, I ascended a mountain as others have done to find refuge, sanctuary, haven, and to solve mystery. I needed courage to scale the mountain and find the nature of my sufferings. Great prophets and men of consciousness secluded themselves to find purpose and meaning. My life had been one of difficulty and trouble, my heart and soul were missing the spirit of love. In this climb, the journey became the cornerstone of my resurrection. I left on that mountain, after I spoke to God, my pain, agony and self-destructive nature. What was attached to me, I left there having regurgitated the entire trauma. I finally walked into the light. My life started a new journey of discovering love, purpose, and me. There is nothing more powerful than love. For me, God is love. I found love was never missing, He was always there.

When I sat down and began this venture into yesterday, I asked myself, "Why go back and script the events which were painful; so many connotations, overtones, and nuances to relive." I had previously started and stopped, not desiring to venture down that road. It is funny how as much as we try to escape what is necessary for our growth and development, it always discovers a way to find us, and urge us onward to fulfillment. The source of our existence loves us. After carefully thinking of undraping myself for others to see, I decided to let my life be an open book. Let it be something of healing and contentment to myself as well as those who may have traveled along a road called pain, like me.

When I was going through decision making, it was always the fear that I struggled with. Fear was always my companion through life and although it has been recognized for what it is, I still permitted the roommate (EGO) in my head to point out in doing something like telling it all – how different my life may become. I contemplated being rejected, those same feelings I grappled with growing up. You see, I made the decision to go forward because there were still splinters in me.

Those small items inside all of us, at times, which irritates at moments and we live with. I have no idea or certainty about what this description of redemption and healing may do. In reality, I am not in control. So the journey to travel back and look at me begins. God's love helped me to survive all those times I was lost at sea, it was God who navigated the course of my existence. It is my obligation to share myself with humanity. This is a necessity and it gives me continued restoration, from a soul once tortured by others to an embodied person who was forgiven. This is my story.

SHARING

I wanted to share my life not only through the words I have scripted, but also through giving some of the proceeds to organizations and religious places of worship. I think it is important that some concerns I have heard, to do something for them. It is not for recognition or to be praised. I have always given more of me. Even in darkness, a little light came out of my heart. I wish I could soak the world of its sorrows and catch the tears of the many who are hurting or in despair. Some of these organizations and people showed me a little kindness and extended themselves for my betterment. The organizations and charities I wish to help are listed below. In purchasing this book I hope you can identify with, but never have to use. I am serious about allowing my life to help transform others. I always wandered seeking my passion in life. I was out of alignment for many years and I am honored to try and honor those who saw something good in me. There is good in everyone, but sometimes the crest of evil conceals our good and divine nature.

Purple R.E.I.G.N. Social Services (domestic violence)
Mildred Phipps Scott Scholarship Foundation
The Allen L. Simpkins, III Foundation

CHAPTER 1
A LITLE BOY NAMED ME

It was hard to forget what was done. All through the night that little boy trying to hide never worked. It always found the little boy with knees pressed to his chest. The little boy tried to yell yet no ear could be found. It told, 'Better not make a sound.' The little boy, now a man, often thinks of why it had to happen to that little boy. When yesterday comes and pays a visit to the man today, it's always a reminder of that little boy named me...who forgave himself...it was NEVER his fault.

In the 1950's the world was much different. Communities were special and lives were valued and honored. It was a speck in time that race was never a deciding factor to me. It only surfaced after me and many others took a bite of the apple and our eyes were opened. Innocence I felt was never again.

As an African-American boy born in the early 1950's, I had no idea the many changes my eyes would see! Wars, assassinations, protests, men walking on the moon, and culture values being challenged and debated. Civil Rights were the focal point of the struggle against years of oppression. It was an America coming of age with a newness that would shape the destiny of many lives; some close to me and others just part of the change.

Mother

My mother, Mildred, was an exquisite woman. Born in 1910 and twice married, she never conceived a child with her husbands. Being a victim of rape at age two and again as a teenager, had her thinking she could not have children. Bizarre, but that is why she thought she was childless. She had me late in life, so in her eyes I was extremely special. She loved my existence and always engaged in adoring and spoiling my nature. She never married my father.

My mother was lovely! She was not a whore nor did she sell herself. She was a hard-working woman with a lot of friends. There was Mr. Billy who never bothered with me, but was my mother's lover at one time. Mr. Jesus, who worked at the VA Hospital with Mom, always fixed my bike. He was nice. Mr. Jones was okay. I think he wanted to just gobble my Mom up! You know how it goes; be nice to the kid to get close to the mother. Then there was Limp Leg George who was great! He had me believe he could drive with no hands until he got into an accident on 125th Street in Harlem. He begged me not to tell my Mom! I obliged his request because I had found someone who lied like me. There was also Mr. "Itchy." I called him that because he had a skin condition that made him scratch all the damn time! My favorite was Mr. Morris; dark as hell with a gold tooth.

He was a hard worker, snappy dresser, was good to Mom and had a new Cadillac every couple years. I used to ride in that Cadillac and it was something special! We rode all over and they would come to get me in New York at summer's end. I told them I was going to steal that car and drive away. But first I was going to line up all the monsters and run them over; back up and run them over again! There were a few others.

Father

My father, Earl Gibson, was 18 years younger than Mom! A West Indian from the Bahamas, I really did not care for him in the beginning. To me, he was just another man; Mother's friend. He was a cavalier and attractive man who dressed well and romanced older women. He and my mother were not married, but he lived not far away in Philadelphia, PA.

He would visit on holidays, and when he did, I was on my best behavior. I was afraid of him. I can recall just wanting him to come and leave as soon as possible. He was moody; like I am at times. When my father visited, he never took me to the park or was interested in what I was doing academically. I mean, he would ask obligatory questions about school, but never in the true sense of a real father. I have come to understand, he probably did not know how. Earl would buy me a few things. I suppose he had an agreement with my mother. Yet, it was my mother who always gave. I was a jewel in her eyes and she spoiled me rotten. Neither of them ever knew what was happening to me behind closed doors!

Me

Born in New York, I was the child of an older single parent. At the time, this was frowned upon, but in my mother's case, never exploited. There was happiness for me as I enjoyed innocence and my loving mother. I recall summer breezes and lightning bugs flying about. The sky looked so different and the quietness of life was well suited for me.

We moved to East Orange, New Jersey when I was a baby; into the home of Mother's former in-laws. It was a huge house on the corner of South Burnett Street and Elmwood Avenue; right across from Vernon L. Davis School. East Orange and society in general, was extremely clean in those days. There also was an abundance of fair-skinned folks. We moved to Orange in the latter half of the 1950's. Mom purchased a house for us on Beach Street in the Valley and I started kindergarten at Forest Street School. This was a mixed ethnic neighborhood with many children. Everyone got along although in some parts of America, racism and a host of other personal bias were evident. I remember the first time someone called me the N word. I fought and kicked a white boy's behind and I did not even know what N was! I just knew I had to defend against how it made me feel. Back then we fought and were friends the next day. As insulting and hurting we sometimes were to each other, we always found room to make friends again. It was a lot different than today. Fist fights are a thing of the past. Young people now shoot one another over the way one may have glanced at the other! Metcalf playground was the great equalizer for the Valley children. All were friends and equal.

I was the only child on Beach Street without a father present in the home and a mother who was older than the mothers of my friends. This disturbed me somewhat. I still recall the shame I initially felt when Mom had to sign my report cards and her name was different than mine. Mom worked at the VA Hospital on Tremont Avenue in East Orange, so after school I would go to the people's house she arranged to watch me. They had two girls and a boy who was a year older than me; my playmate. There are such distinct memories of my world back then. I loved school! There also were the street games played with the other children on Beach Street. Little did I know that the clouds and the beauty I once saw the world through would become dark!

Blindfolded

I was playing in the yard one day with the sky clear and the grasshoppers hopping about on such a nice day. I liked chasing the grasshoppers; I used to pull their legs apart! It was real neat with the sun beaming down upon my head; I did not have a concern in the world. I was a child of innocence with the biggest gap between my teeth. Then I heard the sound of a whistle from my mother's friend, who said, *"Come here for a moment. I have something to show you!"* I walked, tripping over that big old rock in the yard as I stumbled towards a smiling face which appeared safe. I said, *'What is it that you have that you want to show me?'* He said, *"Its inside and it's really neat!"* I walked through the door and did not give it a second thought as he said, *"You have to be blindfolded to see!"* So this funny smelling handkerchief covered my eyes as I heard him say, *"Open wide your mouth for here comes the surprise!"* I felt just like that grasshopper I guess, torn and painful; ripped apart. I left and the sky was black and the dark clouds I saw stayed with me most of my life blindfolded; such fears! You never know what is coming, and really, how can you see.

CHAPTER 2
THE BEGINNING OF DARKNESS

592

The fortress of carnal appears to be serene. Its inhabitants play the role of sanctified people, yet I know they are a fraudulent bunch of carnivores. The person behind the door on the left is the one whom likes to show and doesn't want me to tell; leaving me with an assortment of shame, formulated in a drum of guilt. He has captured me on a few occasions behind the doors of 592 and left me in a state of shock; which everyone thought was my zany ways.

Mr. --- was his name. The one who waited until everyone was subdued to start a fiasco of plundering me. All the times behind 592, I was an experimentation of this person who molested my soul. Mother never knew and I tried to tell her, but she just did not know. Each day she would knock on the door and lead me in for them to watch me, yet it was really an offering of my sacrifice. 592 began my troubles; encompassing my life for years. Never could reveal my burden, it consumed my entire heart. What a tragedy, the moments of me being the prize of some grown-ups conquest of this small son of my loving mother who had no idea what was taking place at 592.

Trauma

My first recollection of trauma happened while in the care of those who watched me while my mother was at work. In describing this time, in no way am I trying to throw harmful implications. I am just expressing how the moments during that time affected me.

The manner of discipline of those who watched me was not good. When their children did bad things, I got whipped too. This was sickening to me. Even the verbal abuse I endured was troubling. I just hated going there every day. I would rebel periodically, yet my mother never asked or investigated my disparity. I was becoming extremely depressed. Possibly, it was unrecognizable.

Mr. was a male housekeeper at the house of the people who kept me early on. He was the one who inserted his perverted behavior into me. He was the one who had me on my knees as a little boy, performing oral sex on him whenever he could capture me. He took advantage of me and my childhood friend (the son of those who watched me). Sometimes he would make me watch while he did things to my friend; terrible things which in my heart, I knew were bad.

Mr. (his name is not important, as he is long gone; dead), was a snake. Cunning, devious and shrewd; I initially thought his playfulness was innocent! He would smile and be so jovial around the adults. Little did I know, he had bad intentions towards me? The first time he molested my spirit and raped my tiny body was when I was five or six years of age. He forced himself on me and my world changed. Sporadically Mr. had me whenever I had to stay and wait for Mother to pick me up. It was always a pinch here or a fondling there. He threatened me somewhat if I was to tell. When our home caught fire, we went to live in the finished basement of 592. At that time, homes had coal chutes. Mr. had me by the furnace. I did not see him coming! Before I knew it, he was on me like a tiger that lays in wait for a surprise attack on its prey. I just laid there and allowed my mind to think of ways I could be dead or in New York with those who protected me. This man had his way over the years and it left me buried in shame and guilt. His perverted behavior was being stitched into me. It was like having filthiness attached at all times. He was a monster! I sometimes wonder how many other boys; and possibly girls, he had his way with.

As a young boy, what could I have done? I was afraid to tell, yet I wanted to kill him. I grew to understand more thoroughly that in the African-American communities there was at that time, a silence about abuse. We were supposed to endure the punishments and traumas inflicted upon us. Because of our history as rejected and despised in this country, we keep whatever abuse that comes our way as 'just a part of life.' I believe that most of the fatalities and toxic behavior we see in urban areas today, is the result of trauma. Whether it's sexual, mental or physical abuse, it is a cancerous seed planted and deeply rooted in our heart and soul.

The painful traumas were causing me to become introverted to some degree. I still was an excellent student, yet my loneliness and painful thoughts were mounting. Because of feelings of inadequacy and confusion, I thought at a very early age of killing myself. In trying to remedy those feelings, I just isolated and went along to get along. These traumas are placed upon children's shoulders and it takes its toll. We begin to demonstrate all sorts of bizarre behavior; becoming destructive to ourselves and others. I thought I was powerless at that age to challenge. Instead, I was becoming increasingly angry toward my mother. Mother depended on those she believed would care for me, not knowing that I was being transformed to a nightmare for society; like many other children of trauma. Being an only child, my Mom gave me more than she should I suppose. I was not appreciative because I was becoming angry. Usually, children of trauma become hurt, and later angry. I had plenty good reasons to me mad.

Captured

Pressure at that time for this child of seven. In the spring of 1960 watching TV; can't remember what. All of a sudden the moment when Mr. surrounded me. Did not know this game. He pushed me on my knees. Began a tragedy. It hurt me so bad; never was the same. I did not like that game. It took years to work through that moment of my captivity.

Harlem

I used to spend summers in New York with my Little Mama. She and my Mom were like sisters. We lived on 142nd Street between 7th and Lenox Avenues before we moved to New Jersey. Little Mama took care of me while my Mom worked at Bellevue Hospital. Later on they used to say I was the way I was because I came from the crazy hospital! I think Little Mama resented when Mom moved to New Jersey. People had convinced her it was the best move. I look at it now and say, 'Thank God she moved!'

I loved New York. I felt relieved from the abuse I was caught up in. In New York I could run in the streets and go to the Apollo Theater with my cousin Mildred; it was Ronald, Michael, Mildred, and me. I loved being with them. I felt safe. I used to even eat the crabs for a dime and go swimming in Colonial Pool which has been renamed on 145th and St. Nicolas. I also was involved with the Minisink Camp who took us to Bear Mountain and host of events. They were located on Lenox Avenue up from the 364th Armory. Each time I went to New York there was something new to learn.

My Little Mama connected me with guys around my age. There was Dwight, George Lee, Clyde, and Bernard. I learned how to play handball and it was just different. We ran through the backyard between the buildings trying to slingshot cats and dogs. As crazy as it sounds it was fun. I hated to go back to New Jersey when my mother and Mr. Morris used to come pick me up. I would cry not so much for leaving as to being carted back to the abuse I hated.

The most devastating loss I felt in my life was the death of my cousin Ronald. I did not understand why this happened or the reason why he died at that time. It was a traumatic experience for everyone. I learned when I was a little older the cause of his death; an overdose of heroin. I remember when my mother's house caught fire, Ronald came over. I peeked through a window and saw him and a young lady sticking a needle in their arm. I did not know then that my own life would turn for the worse, and I too, would indulge in the dangerous game of drugs as a heroin user. My Mother was upset because Ronald loved her a lot; called her *"Fats."* It was told that as a young boy he questioned why Little Mama's breasts were not like my Mom's!

Those were happier times. The tragedy was, he had just come home that morning from rehab and left the house. The next thing Little Mama knew, someone knocked on the door and informed her "Chink" (Ronald's nickname) was on the roof dead. He stayed on that roof from that morning until that night; dead. It still hurts! Little Mama, Michael and I guess Mildred, never recovered from Chink's death.

Michael would soon take on a lifestyle similar to his brother because he could not get past the loss. For me, it was yet another trauma. I felt like throwing in the towel, so to speak. All life seemed to present to me was pain and suffering. There were liberated moments, but suffering seemed to be the majority shareholder on my life.

The day of the funeral, everyone tried their best to conceal their pain. All of Chink's friends were there. I used to love watching them get their hair processed and wrapped up. Daniels Funeral Parlor on 132nd Street in Harlem, I believe, held the service. We then moved to the Bronx where his final resting place would be. The remarkable thing about that day was when they let his pigeons loose. Ronald used to fly birds and would take me on the roof plenty of times to see the birds soaring. I even remembered the last time I saw him alive. He took me with him to see *Splendor in the Grass* at the Roosevelt Theater on 145th and 7th Avenue; and made me walk all the way down 142nd Street where he lived alone. I was proud of myself, but scared. Well these birds took off and by the time we were home, the birds were on the fire escape! I still recall that thrilling experience!

Pain

The year 1963 was just terrible for me. The loss of Ronald; and then came another tragedy which not only affected me, but the country as a whole. President John F. Kennedy was assassinated that November. It was loss once again and left me with the feeling at my young age that life was painful and upsetting. I remember sitting and watching the whole event on TV. The killing seemed to rip America's heart. This man was loved by so many, especially Blacks – it was like we were killed too. In any case, I again found reason to regress into my world of depression. Everyone was glued to the TV and I found refuge pressing my knees to my chest in fear again and again. I still remember the President's horse-drawn carriage as it proceeded down Pennsylvania Avenue and his son saluting his casket! Black folks did not know what would happen as far as their fight for civil/human rights were concerned. I have no idea why, but I felt like I wanted to die, too. At the least, I hoped the world would just ignore my presence. It was a year I will recall until I exit this world.

Not only did my initial monster have his way, but there were others of my mother's friends who started to search me out with that false smile. You see, my mother was a good person and our house was a place where people came and drank their Four Roses and Calvert liquor. I hated the fact they were always in my house. After a while when the intoxication would settle in, I could hear them instructing my mother about what to do with me; or, *"You know you had that boy too late in life."*

There was Ms. E who was just a bully. She bullied my mother. My Mom had soft ways. Her gentleness was often taken for weakness. Ms. E. also resided at 592. Regardless the conversation, she would be loud and obnoxious. She always thought she was right about this or that and was the leader of destroying my character. Every time she saw me she had something negative to say to me. There was no encouragement or motivation just, *"Butch ain't shit and never going to be shit."* I despised her and thought she was nothing but a she-devil. She would always start some crap and it came to a point where I would hate to see her coming. It was always something to degrade me. It was not discipline; it was her unhappiness with herself. I did not know why at the time, but I disliked her existence and the way she bossed my mother. It is something about learned behavior that passes along, where one can find them doing exactly what was done to them. When I got older, maybe 12 or 13, I took pleasure in punishing this woman. I would wait like a vulture until she became drunk and argumentative and needed help to get home. This was my chance to get even!

I would do to her the same things which were done to me. When I helped her home, she would plop on the bed and act as if she were sleep. She would half-heartedly swat me away, but then would kick her legs open. The perverse ways that were stitched into me, I would experiment on her. I cursed her out and felt in control. It was difficult pulling her pajamas off so I, in my zeal, would just cut them off. I sometimes sit today and shake my head at the craziness I was a part of. You see, I was becoming someone with deep behavior issues. I knew I was becoming bizarre; and it did not just stop with Ms. E. I would prey on others who sat in my mother's home drinking as well.

I assumed the role of predator. I started hating my existence and unhappiness was buried in me. I wore this image when I played in the street or engaged in sports. I was lonely and felt unprotected and expendable – did not matter whether I lived or died. I even tried over and over again to get up the courage to kill myself only to back out. I cut my shoulder with a razor deliberately, although not deep. I just took slices to prepare for my wrists one day.

The craziness continued behind closed doors. I believe in African-American households we are prepared early on to suffer through pain and to just allow ourselves to hurt. I thought maybe it was because of our slave experience, where we just sopped it up and adopted an 'it is what it is' stance. I continued to find refuge in solitude whenever I could find it. I was an extraordinary student; gifted and talented. I always had the ability to exceed. I was an honor student.

By 1965, I was ashamed and felt a tremendous amount of guilt. I cried and masked it by still trying to uphold that I was okay. Inside I was in turmoil. What I did not understand was why I was so fearful of everything deep down inside. I felt insufficient. The suit of pain given to me was excruciating. I used to always hide somewhere where I could not be found. I sat in corners undetected in my solitude. I hated myself for the fear I felt and I despised people for who they were. I still played sports and other games with the guys on my street. Some of these guys were, and are to this day, still my friends. They knew of my plight to some degree. Most people I just categorized as monsters that only used my mother or those who could not wait to catch me alone and have their way with me.

Chiseled

Sculptors of madness, chipping away on me, their eyes closed in sequence as they take their turns on me. Nowhere to run, nowhere to hide – they seek me out to chisel a mother's son. Why? Exertion as they strangled the very innocence

> *with me, leaving me sculptured in shame and guilt. Someone please push me over and break me in pieces.*

Mr. L. and Mr. W. worked with my mother at the hospital. Mr. L. had his eyes on me from the gate. Every time at parties where everyone attended, including the children, he would find a way to pinch or touch me as if to say *'hello.'* What he was really saying was, *'I'm going to get you!'* Every day it seemed new monsters appeared. I saw the real looks of these people. They may have smiled and laughed, but I saw their demons watering at the mouth; waiting to pounce upon me. Mr. L. finally captured and performed oral sex on me. I thought at the time that this was usual, so what the hell. He would give me a couple of bucks. Strangely, I accepted the money and went about my way. I was starting to prostitute myself. I did not care. I just went along! This new policy became ratified in my life with my willingness to participate. Every time there was company in our home, I would brace myself in a dark corner. I knew someone would make their way to my room and assault me.

By the time 1966 came, I started doing what I wanted. I was moving off the chart. I was still subject to violation but I was also changing. When I was alone I would be deep in depression at times. I would hide with my knees pressed to my chest; crying because of the change which was overtaking me. I also started to sample the drinking they left in their glasses. I was a candidate, I believe, for the lifestyle I was to lead. I am this smiling kid who was wearing a mask.

I talked to my mother something awful. I was blaming her inside for what was happening to me. I never told her directly, yet my conversation warranted an investigation, but she never looked in the right direction. I was going insane and my thought process was becoming anti-social and a host of other analogies. My mother started having me see a psychologist who never got to the root of my suffering. Lines were so blurred and skewed for me back then, that I would become a great liar. I could talk a good game and had a gift of persuasion. I was convincing; a true thespian. It was easy to fool the psychologist. No one knew why I started to slowly crumble. It did not happen all at once. It should be understood I had a choice in my life to do many things positively; but because of my thinking, I always lived in fear. Fear of whatever I put in my head to be afraid of. I always wanted to die. I tried to commit suicide as I mentioned, but was a coward I presume. Like the time I was going to jump into a pond about three feet down. What a joke! I even tried cutting myself to no avail. I still bear the cut marks on my shoulders today.

I continued to break into pieces. Stealing from my mother was the easiest. I started doing things I supposed young kids do, but my self-esteem was going downward. The people who kept me ruled my mother's life, I thought, and I began to curse everybody. In my mind I was protecting my mother but it was explained to her that something was wrong with me. They always verbally abused me until I actual thought I was filthy. African-Americans in my neighborhood had a tendency to do things which were abusive and everybody turned their heads like nothing was happening. I just rebelled. Besides my athletic ability, I was heading into an intersection of destruction. My monsters were still around and I was participating in unsavory actions. My thoughts were perverted and instead of being focused, all my thoughts were on ways to cause havoc to myself and others. I wanted others to feel pain! Anything I could do to be an ass, I did. My Mom was my biggest target.

Mother's Friends

My mother had a host of friends as I mentioned. Some were her friends and some were just in our lives to cause havoc. I have learned over years that there are some people who no matter what, do not have your best interest at heart. I guess what disturbed me the most was my mother's quantity of male friends and quality of both male and female friends. There were those who just wanted my mother to throw me in a pot of boiling water if it were possible and then there were those who were genuine. Yet the constant badgering of what to do with me or what kind of child I was, bothered me so much. I was not a kind child because I felt protective of my mother and I usually would argue with adults at my young age. So the word went out about my behavior. Little did anyone understand the hardship I was experiencing was because of the trauma. I was angry as hell and I started to become more and more unraveled. Sometime during puberty, I would become a predator myself. It became a game for me to seek out my mother's female friends and have my young way with them. I sometimes wonder, did they know what I was doing to them, or were they truly asleep? In any case, I was all over the place and well on my way to becoming a monster.

Mr. W. showed up when I was about 13-years old. I used to see him when I went to the VA Hospital to beg money from my Mom. Mother introduced me to another monster for sure. The difference is, when he started coming to the house for drinks, I would walk through with an attitude of not caring. He would give me the look of, *'I'd like to get you somewhere!'* We all know the looks people give us to see if there is an opening. I paid it no mind until I escalated my drug use and needed money. I was near the local bar in the Valley when I saw him and he offered me money to have oral sex. I never gave it a second thought as to whether this is wrong or should I tell. I just did not care about living or dying at that point. I was suicidal and did anything and everything to release me from my pain.

Mr. W. lived upstairs from my godmother on Tremont Avenue in Orange. I had to be careful, but once again, I was doing bad things because I had no sense of value or self-worth and I, who could prostitute me without hesitation. This relationship with him was whenever there was a shortage of getting drug money. Most insulting was my Mom thought these people were innocent and nice. I used to blame her, but she never knew that early on I was a vessel for those monsters who thought this young boy needed to be raped. She also, for a while, was unaware I was shooting drugs. There is a picture I have where I am all smiles with my Mom. Then there is another with a stern look on my face of hating the world and everything in it. I never saw Mr. W. after I moved on. He was like all the others who inflicted pain in my life. I take full responsibility for my part. I may have been vulnerable as a lad of five or six, but as a teenager I knew exactly what I was doing; I had a choice. There were many times when propositions showed-up during my drug infested life. If I got sick, I would participate in out-of-ordinary behavior. I was not a friend. I strolled through life looking for and distributing pain upon those who either loved me, or was in the way.

Behind Closed Doors

Amazing how I wished night time would never come back in the days of old, for I felt a little safer in the daylight away from those doors which closed and the rampage would start with real monsters locking me into a tailspin of shame. Behind closed doors, so much happened which sculptured a part of my life, taking me through channels of insanity to alleyways of infested surroundings, all because of the guilt I felt. Behind closed doors where my mouth was covered so no one could hear this child of blamelessness screaming and my tiny heart beating, I was so much afraid, asking myself why this was happening to me. All I wanted was this massacre to stop behind those closed doors. Behind closed doors back then the anguish I felt, unhappiness became my direction I had no self-esteem, I felt so dirty not at all clean back then after the monsters had their way behind those closed doors. My life took a drastic turn all because of what happened to me behind closed doors. We aren't supposed to tell so I carried pain for so many years. I was a young Black male child raped by those who were supposed to be my mother's friends watching me behind closed doors. It's strange, how all the years I dwelled in obscurity and loneliness I couldn't accept my trauma for what it was; pain.

Girls

There were girls my age I liked and I even stole my mother's jewelry to give to CL. I do not want to mention her name but being young, I loved this ponytailed neighbor of mine. She had a lot of sisters and appeared mixed – Hispanic I presumed. They all had Spanish names. The funny thing is I used to steal my mother's jewelry to give to her. I was always a giving person. I guess it came from wanting to fit in. Buying my way for people to accept me or let me be a part of; and this behavior of giving my last, transcended most of my life. Even later on I used to just give all my clothes away just so I would be liked. My self-esteem and what I felt about myself was low.

This young lady Ms. CL, was a princess to me. I sat and dreamed about her and me running away and finding refuge on an island of innocence. My puppy love for her was overwhelming and everyone knew she was my prize. We never engaged in anything sexual. We were kids, and I just loved her in my childish way. We all have our first love as children that we find happiness and fulfillment. I felt as though I had an idea of what caring was about because it had to be different from what I was experiencing from my captors. Ms. CL's father was an undertaker and boy-oh-boy, was everyone scared of this guy! He used to park his hearse in front of their house and go inside for extended periods with a body in the car! My friends and I would sneak up to the car and peak in and see someone strapped down and covered. I was scared but wished it was me.

Years later Ms. CL and I talked about back then and I confessed what Mr. had done to me. Left his signature upon me contributing to the anguish I would carry through a great deal of my life. She indicated he had tried to get her too, but she ran and told her father who threaten to kill Mr. if he ever touched her. I thought to myself I wish someone had protected me. The thing is I did not tell! I kept it all bottled up inside, and I was afraid he may have hurt my mother and isolate her. You see, my mother thought she needed all these people, for what reason I have no idea. She felt as though if she got in trouble or sick these were the only people to help her. Bottom-line, these people did not have her interest at heart. They talked to her like she was in a cotton field at times. Ms. CL and I still see each other from time-to-time. When I see her, in my mind's eye, she is still running around with her shorts and white socks and pigtails. God bless her existence and she will always be dear to me; her and me together on an island of innocence away from life's hardships.

There was another young lady who also gave me reason to be hopeful. She was a lovely angel my eyes saw one day at Tremont Avenue School in Orange, New Jersey. I just thought she was someone who I could love. She looked at me with caring eyes. She made me feel whole. Our encounter of becoming acquainted was after a basketball game between Tremont and Central Schools. She was standing on Main Street and had on those white go-go boots and she had the finest bowlegs I thought God had ever created. We knew we liked one another. She was a grade higher than me. She was an enigma someone in my own madness that would run away with me to a life of joy and happiness. She lived in a section of Orange where affluent people resided. Her father was in a biracial marriage and back in those days it was still uneasiness. I doubt they could have lived as freely if they lived in the south or even in some parts of New Jersey. Few communities anywhere would have tolerated such a union.

Evelyn was her name! I used to walk her to Berkeley Avenue in Orange and we would just stand there, talking and kissing. I wanted to have sex with her and I believe if I had pushed the envelope we would have engaged. There were days when she would want me to go a little further, but I was afraid. We could have gone to my house during lunch time and experimented, but it never happened. Part of it was I wanted to save her until we were married which is noble in some respect, but in reality I was afraid. I did not know how to engage because of fear. I was so used to those elder monsters that were having sex with me, that someone in my own age bracket, made it difficult. I understand now that my thoughts and the fear had caused me to have these feelings. How could I explain to her the inadequacies I felt? How could I put forth to her the defects I felt inside as a teenager? How could I divulge my innermost shame and guilt? I was stuck. I really liked and loved her. Being with her was my salvation and freedom.

As soon as I left her my emptiness shrouded me. She has no idea today of how much I respected her and thought she was my source of freedom. I also knew of her unhappiness with her stepmother. It had to be difficult for her because it is not like today where mixed marriages are a commonality. She was unhappy inside; I now can see. We were two young people who were in pain. Pain attracts pain and we cried on each other's shoulder each and every day. She had a scar on her cheek which made her to me, so beautiful. Most people may have looked at this as a negative; I always thought she was beautiful. She had her own insecurities I am sure about that scar.

Well, we drifted along looking forward to standing on that corner. I never walked her to her door, being things were the way they were. Even now as I pass that corner, and it has been close to 47 years ago, I can still feel her and me. I can pull over and reminiscence and think about the moments we had. I ask myself today, what would have happened if we would have had sex. What differences would have been made? Even today she has no idea of how much I cared for her. Was it an infatuation, possibly – but she may never know that she gave me freedom, for a sequence in time. Every time I walked her home it was like soaring somewhere over the radiances of beauty. Just for the moment I could hold someone who did not make me feel dirty or ashamed. My anguish was gone for a moment and my mind became civil and I rested inside. She was and will always be special to me.

Even today if I were to see her I would feel genuine because of what she gave me. She may look upon my comments with amusement and smile. Out of all the failings I felt within, she was the only source of liberation for me. This freedom lasted a school day each and every day. She went to high school and our journey together ended. My friends used to ask me if I had got it as they used to say (had sex) with her; and back then you did not want to be a square so I would lie. I would act a certain way around my friends concerning her, but her and I never had sex. Was there opportunities, yes and I believe she wanted me to. She was in pain emotionally as I mentioned and this could have been a release I am sure for the two of us, but I was afraid and felt that it would take away the purity of the way I felt towards her.

When she went to high school and I still remained in grammar school, the intensity of my shame and guilt increased. Even when we were a couple, as soon as I left her presence I found some stupidity to get myself into; drugs or engaging in abnormal behavior. I was always up to no good in one way or another. I recall that when she left, I felt abandoned and became upset when she found new relationships to explore. Someone did what I would not do. In reality that is the way it is in life. People seek out that which brings the pleasure and pain. She sought out new friends and new relationships which I presume had its ups and downs. There was a moment when some guys were making comments about her. It was in the old field house at Bell Stadium. I used to go there with RW who was an extremely great athlete in high school. Anyhow, they were asking me questions about her and I played naïve. Then they started to say what one of the guys who were going with her had said he was doing. I caught an attitude and really felt my whole world being crushed. More traumas! I just could not understand that in some respects, this had nothing to do with me. I had my time with her.

Why was I so upset? This is one example how I could not accept things in my life. Events usually dismantled me and I became soaked in sorrow. In my mind I was crushed. I could not decipher whether I was upset because I felt she was mine or that someone else may have been having sex with her. Nevertheless, I took myself through something and this was another excuse to act out. I have always felt a bonding with her. As I mentioned I was only free emotionally with her. I felt safe and she always made my heart smile. She is one of a few who never tried to hurt me. Even after I went to high school and used to see her, she was always courteous, polite, and when she saw me made brief conversation.

I can still remember when she told me she was pregnant. She never knew how devastated I was. She never knew how emotionally unsound I was when she got married. I was happy for her and upset inside. This fantasy feeling that I constructed in my mind, as though she was mine, was my own madness. Like I said, I think because of her softness, attractiveness, wonderful heart and soul towards me, I always felt her in so many ways. I saw her from time-to-time after she married and would hear things concerning her life. Even though some things I heard may not have been enjoyable to hear, I would never say anything negative about her. Even after all these years, she is still someone that takes me there, somewhere near a field of tenderness, where the world's troubles have no meaning. She is an enigma of sort. I say this because out of all the plundering I was going through, she was an outlet, someone each and every day in school and after school the world seemed to become a little bit more to grasp. In my eyes there were only a few who gave me a reason to want to understand and live. She was one of them.

I received an e-mail one day and I responded in an annoyed way. It was a chain letter kind of thing. I acted very nasty, like do not bother me with this crap. Upon closer scrutiny, I noticed her name in the list of persons receiving this letter. I shot her an e-mail asking if she was the same E from my home town! She responded, *"Yes,"* even though she did not know yet who was asking. I was blown away! It was like Stanley finding Livingston in Africa, or hearing from someone you never in a million years thought you would be speaking to. We connected and she informed me she was doing some work in the New Jersey area. I wanted to see her and something inside wanted her to see how my life had changed. I wanted to just go back to that corner. I went where she was working and it was the happiest moment of my life. This is another time she never knew how much I enjoyed being in her grace. She was a part of my early formative years. I saw her a couple of times after that and she went back out of state to live. I believe she was commuting anyway. She is and will always be special. It is like having something that really makes you feel good come into your thoughts and your heart begins to serenade you. I wish her nothing but the best. Funny how I always found a way to throw her into the other young ladies and women I engaged within my life whenever there was a conversation about my past. By the time I came out of my daydreaming and talking about her I usually would have to argue. I must have made her too real. Lady Evelyn, thank you for what you gave to me not knowing the hell I was living with. Best wishes.

The Fellas

We played all the games kids participated in. There was Allen, Cut, J, and the white kids on the street. J and his sisters were the kids of the people who watched me. I was a good athlete even back then. I played Pop Warner football and used to enjoy going to the high school games. Because I was a good sportsman, the older guys would allow me to play with them. There was a guy named Joe who we named Dino. He looked like Fred Flintstone so we decided to name him after that dinosaur. He was big. It is a funny thing about back in the day everything looked huge. Even the hallways were like walking in some monumental palace. Dino used to be the quarterback and he would throw me the ball when we played on the street. He used to take me to the track meets and football games at Bell Stadium. Eventually, we got into the drug game together. Allen and I would play pick-up games of basketball behind Our Lady of the Valley Church until the wee hours of the morning.

Dear Allen,

There are many things I never got a chance to say to you. When you made your transition, I was late getting to your services. I was trying to kill myself earlier on that day. I wanted to say to you when you first became ill; I never came to see you because I did not want to experience something happening to you. I was fragile and was totally living on the wild side. I have no excuse other than my own selfish nature taking control of me. I just was not stable. I cried so much in losing you. I was in NY in an abandoned building getting high. Someone said in this setting, "If anyone overdoses, they going out the window." I did not care at all. I was so distraught because I always felt I had abandoned you. You were my friend and the pain of your death took many years for me to come to terms with. Please forgive me for not being there the many times you may have needed me. – Coo

A Hat that Never Fits

I bring to light my quest for seeking answers trying to understand why. I had tried many formulas trying to make sense of my purpose and why I have only found a temporary, passing wind, or a provisional meaning wherever I searched. The hat never fit...

When I found myself in arenas where I thought numbing me was the way to avoid the pain of everyday living because my question wasn't resolved, I recalled being isolated as a child with emptiness as my companion...it has always been vacuums of never-ending hollowness...the hat never fits...

Trying religion became a pointlessness of segregation, apartheid, and ghettoization...the hat never fits...As I sat listening to yesterday's stories of myths and fantasies...fire and brimstone dialogues with me knowing the hat once again didn't fit...

I wandered across the earth only finding unpleasantness as so many wanted to make a hat fit for me...Everything I sought was only my inability to trust me...love me...and to come to terms with maybe, just maybe...finding a hat that fits...may not be necessary...Yet until then I am uncertainty, an indecision maker, and vagueness, a prisoner of my own madness I ran away from life...seeking death all because of wanting hats that never fit.

CHAPTER 3
JOINING THE CIRCUS

Clown School

I knew better about the way I behaved, I just no longer cared. All that happened to me brought about baggage which one day would damn near kill me. My saga is overwhelming. Maybe I had to go through what I did to become who I am today. I still question why. What I do understand today is why it is important for me to expose what happened to me. I was concerned about how others would perceive me after reading my story. I wrote it anyway, because it is about healing and making whole that which evaporated on the banks of hardship brought about by those who did to me what most likely was done to them. This cycle of learned behavior is difficult to understand. We pass along pain and trauma to others as if spreading a cold. We cough our pervasions and trauma onto others as if gifting them a part of the pain that was instilled in ourselves.

The process of degeneration works the same as any other educational process; daily reinforcement. As mentioned, I lived this double life. I truly enjoyed at one time attending school. I entered Forest Street School 1957 or 1958. It was an integrated school and a lot of my classmates were of different ethnic backgrounds. In school I exceled tremendously; throughout I can recall how I did my work in class and how much I enjoyed being a student. The educational process was much different than today. Neighborhoods were solidified and everyone seemed to know the direction to go. Somewhere over time, with the breakdown of family structure, came the nightmares of the educational school system. Erosion of family structure created the same nightmares in the classrooms of debauchery.

J. and his sisters were the children of the people who watched me early on. As stated earlier, when they did something wrong, I got beat too. Each would share in the wrong the other did. *"All your asses are going to get beat!"* Adults sometimes cannot control their emotions. Many times today we see children killed for no better reason than they were crying too much.

I had always drunk what was left in the glass after the adults had their fun. My Little Mama used to give me a little beer early on. There is a theory that people are candidates for all sorts of behavior patterns long before they act on them. The attitude is established and the immediate gratification comes along and off to the races. I started off drinking wine called Thunderbird. By 1966 I knew how to take the train and get to Harlem on my own. I took a friend over by the name of RT and we, along with my cousin Michael, got pretty high drinking Thunderbird wine on the upper stair casing in the building. It seemed all my pain was gone. I felt invincible and really bold; not caring – little did I know, I would chase those feelings for so many years of my life. The chase had begun and from that first time of crossing the line, I never came back to any reality. I started to dwell in a world where disregard for oneself became my calling. I really tried my best to erase the pain of abuse and other factors from my life. I mean, here I was 12 or 13-years old involved in drinking and drugging. My father who I disliked from my own stuff, gave me permission to smoke in 1966. I started out with Lucky Strikes and Pall Mall's. Eventually, I switched to Kool, which was synonymous with my nickname.

How I got the name Kool, I have no idea! Later, it was shortened to "Coo." People still see me today and greet me with *"Hey Coo!"* I guess I did think I was Kool or some sort of great person. Inside, I hated everything about myself. I hated my height and the slumping of my shoulders. I still did not understand why I was not telling my Mom what they were doing to me. My self-esteem was gone. I was established as a liar who could not be trusted and did not respect his mother. I just knew if I opened my mouth and directly confronted my tormentors, they would have convinced my mother to put me away. By the way; that was discussed from time to time!

This reminds me of an incident that happened in my mother's home. My mother bought a house for little or nothing in 1961, I believe, which had an upstairs apartment. After the house was restored from the fire, a family with a little daughter moved into the upstairs apartment. The little girl must have been two or three-years younger than me; I was about nine years old. On Sunday's she would be dressed to go to Sunday school. While her mother was still getting dressed she would come downstairs. At nine-years old, I wanted the mother! I wanted to do to the mother what was being done to me. She was beautiful! I used to forget my key on purpose so she could come down the stairs, open the door, and as she went back upstairs and I could see up under her nightgown. I used to masturbate all the time thinking about her. Funny I always thought I was the only young boy who did this to himself. Her daughter would come down and I would do the pinching and other things which were being done to me. I would offer her candy just to get a feel.

Finally, on two occasions, I got her on my mother's bed and pulled up her Sunday dress and grinded her, never penetrating. My mother had one of those partitions to close-off the room. Well, I had made up my mind I was going to penetrate her the last time I played this nasty game, the same nasty game other's played with me. She was six or seven and I was nine. I was pulling down her panties and her mother opened that shade and that was it. I can still hear her scream and my pleas not to tell. *'Please don't tell.'* I was not old enough to threaten her to not tell – and when the street found out, that was it. I was marked for life. It was all over the place. The way everyone looked at me now was disturbing. It was like, *"We told you Mildred! Something is extremely wrong with Butch!"* My captors kind of enjoyed when they heard. It was as if they were saying, *"That's my boy! Glad you're becoming one of us!"* I was ashamed again over the progression of my mental instability.

That family moved out of the apartment in a hurry. Over the years when I would see them, I could see the hatred in this little girl's mother's eyes. I avoided the confrontation. I knew she harbored feelings of dislike towards me. I found out later in life that this little girl with the yellow dress on died of complications due to AIDS. I immediately started having feelings about her death. I wondered whether I had traumatized her at that young age where she was made to feel like I felt, and started living a destructive lifestyle. This, along with the many other situations, was something which haunted me and caused me to make unwise choices. The years came and the patterns of negative experimentation continued. Congratulate me! I have graduated clown school.

Couldn't Tell
It's easy for those sitting on the edge to question why you did not tell about the incidents in your life, which brought you a bag full of trauma. Well I wish

it had been that easy for this ratchet soul of the years gone by. Yet my inner self decided to not divulge the evidence of my shame and guilt, which occupied me for so long, dictating my demise whispering 'it's all your fault.' The layers of pushing my feelings aside began to pile up and became harden by my refusing to deal with myself. I was walking around hurting holding up in dwellings; crying my heart out. I dare not say what took place on those days when the real boogieman stole me and raped my heart. Those who shake their head and feel my words probably can identify with where I'm coming from. It leaves you so messed up when you witness over and over again the act, which turned back your clock inside of your bleeding heart. It was ripped out held before me, daring, intimidating my innocent soul. If you are reading this script, know I wanted to tell but couldn't. Was I supposed too? I guess yes, yet my lips stayed quiet while the implant of evil was placed in me nearly killed my spirit sending me out of my body and soul. Well I hope those in this situation will try to tell, and not carry the baggage it takes to go through life subjecting yourself to all sorts of inclinations which those around you wonder what is wrong with you. Take this suggestion; give up the secret tapes, those tapes you said you would take to your grave before you would tell. Rid yourself as I have and spit it up. I felt good to let you know!

The 60's and Drugs

There was something unraveling about the 1960's. In the latter 60's era, things really became even more out of control. The country was in the paradigm shift between the Vietnam War, the protests and the drugs, and I began to sink further into demise. I sometimes think the urban areas were sleep during this awakening period. Injustice was being challenged and people wanted change.

I was introduced to marijuana in New York in 1967. I became lively after a joint or a few drinks. I would tell jokes out of the bathroom window across the buildings to my cousin's neighbors while laughing my ass off! I would do all kinds of crazy antics! My Aunt knew something was wrong, but oh well; I enjoyed the hell out of it! The one thing about my addiction; I was a pest no matter what I had in me.

When I returned to New Jersey, I brought some reefer with me to introduce to the guys my age. I showed them how to roll a joint using a teabag. In my own craziness I thought I was now important. How disturbing my thoughts were. My transition into the drug game was fast. Between 1968 and 1971 I will say everyone was getting high that I knew. In '68 I went up to the roof and my life really changed forever. When I used to go up there with Dino, Larry, my cousin Michael and a few other guys, they would make me wait on the landing below, even though I suspected what they were doing. I wanted to do what they were doing. There used to be arguments amongst them as whether to allow me to participate. They had elevated the ways and means to nullify the pain. I was introduced to heroin. They gave me a bag to sniff. The first time I sniffed a bag of heroin I went to a world beyond anything I had ever experienced before in my life. This was more pain relieving than drinking and smoking reefer. This was the ultimate! I thanked the Lord for sending me what I truly needed! All my pain all the suffering from the abuse and everything that bothered me, evaporated in the moment. I loved it! I adored it! I found my salvation. I crossed the line for sure. I was truly Kool knocking on the door of insanity.

I enjoyed this venture into the negative. The climate in the country was in an uproar and I said to myself, *'what the hell.'* The neighborhoods were being flooded with drugs. I recall how I admired those who sold drugs or were into the numbers game or anything which went against the principles of clean living. There were the slick cars, clothing, and the conversation which amounted to a bunch of crap. Do not get me wrong, there were a lot of individuals who could have been brilliant in another lifetime or if they were doing things in a positive manner. I have been around some geniuses; they were caught like me in a tailspin of insanity. I remember the way we dressed and knowing the hippest people were the thing. Everyone had a vice of some sort.

I found myself wanting to do more than sniff drugs. I wanted to do what the guys I hung out with were doing. My cousin Michael had the drugs. In New York the drugs were cheaper than in New Jersey. You would get a bundle for $20 to $25; there would be 15 bags in a bundle. Each bag was $2.00 in New York. In New Jersey it was 2 for $7, 3 for $11, and 4 for $16. It went on and on like this. I was starting to feel a part of something. Something stupid and dangerous in reality, but in my insane thoughts, I was a part of a corporation. I was unraveling piece-by-piece. My mother just shook her head and wept. Later on she would see me shooting drugs into my arm. She fainted. I did my best to convince her she was dreaming.

Though it would not take long for me to start tying up my own arm, but first skin-popping began. Skin-popping was taking the needle and just shooting the drugs under the skin. Mainlining was shooting directly in the vein. I can still close my eyes and play the tape back of that first encounter. The drugs were strong back then. It was not the chemically-based pharmaceutical affects we have today. I was asked was I sure I wanted to do this. You see, I had been petitioning like a politician running for office to give me the opportunity. How stupid I was when I think about it today. I wanted to relieve myself of the pain I was going through and most of all wanted to be a part of something. I guess it is like gang members today who seek love and acceptance in the wrong corridors of life. I too wanted to be accepted.

I always had that people pleasing perspective. I would do anything to be accepted while seeking other's approval. I began my journey and it was the beginning of a spiral down effect where I nearly destroyed myself. Everything God had created in me I did my best to devastate, damage, and wipe out. I was designated to help move the drugs from New York to New Jersey because of my age. We would catch the number 2 or 3 train from 145th Street right near the bridge to go into the Bronx all the way to 42nd Street. Then we would take the 118 bus to Newark and then the 24, 23 or 44 bus. We would set-up shop in my mother's house and it was like something new; like I was some sort of underworld participant. Little did I know at the time that most of the behavior I was exhibiting was a result of the hatred I had for myself and those whom I blamed.

I started to want to take on the characteristics of those who I thought were role models. Walking as though I was slick, head cocked to the side and speaking with a junkie drawl; even scratching my brains out to emulate a full-fledged junkie became my routine. The inadequacies I felt still dictated my existence. Why not end it all and kill myself, became my foremost thought. Sometimes my memories of pain would flood my mind. I needed a way to solve my inner suffering. The drugs would numb me, but they never distanced me from thinking about Mr. and him blindfolding me. As I strapped up my arm in anticipation of the rush of heroin, my mind drifted as it always did. As my vein is punctured, the video starts playing in the yard one day with the sky clear and the grasshoppers hopping about.

Reliving moments like this allowed me to medicate. There were so many situations where I was handled unbecoming and improper ways. There were other times where I thought so less of myself that I did not care one way or another. I was a candidate for a lifestyle indecent; incorrect, and my heart was blackened. There was no honesty in me.

Malcolm, Martin and Civil Rights

These were two figures who I did not have real regard for because I so caught-up in my world of fantasy and destruction. When Malcolm was killed I was being intentionally fractured by those who did not care. There are dark moments when silence is full of fear and your heart begins to pound because you realize something will soon clutch you and implement pain.

My world was so far and beyond what Malcolm stood for. His manhood, as Ossie Davis quoted during his funeral, never reached me in a positive way or fashion. Those who came up with the idea I would be a vessel of sort, were not men of any value or significance. Malcolm reached across the world with his stand on human rights; yet I and many others were being ravaged upon not by whites, but our own people who had not an inch of manhood or honesty in them.

With Martin, I was sitting on my mother's couch when word came of his assassination. I was cooking-up some drugs and we decided to get blasted. I needed another excuse to not deal with reality and this was the perfect moment. We decided to go back to New York City as soon as possible in case there was a riot – maybe we could benefit. This outrageous thought is what was formed in my mind! Here is a man who sacrificed his own life for the betterment of my living conditions as well as others and all I could think about was plundering and ransacking. I will say, I never knew the real significance of any kind of struggle until my life changed. I sat and saw the Civil Rights era come and the brutality of its markings. Yet I felt brutalized and treated cruel by those who smiled and sat and ate at my kitchen table. I did not have to look towards Alabama, Mississippi, or Georgia to see and feel viciousness. It was in my kitchen or where I may be dropped off at as a kid; so I had always felt abandoned. A derelict is supposed to be someone who has abandoned themselves. I sure left myself after being sectioned out as prey. I sometimes look at the pictures of myself and can still see the façade I wore. How strange the whole picture appeared to be. I truly thought I was worthless and all along I was becoming a monster.

Angry

My mother and I had a peculiar relationship. I can still recall how devilish and bizarre I was towards her. I think my disappointment came when she left me on so many occasions to travel. You see, my mother was an extremely lovely woman. I never really knew exactly how beautiful she was until after she died and I found many photos of her in the late 1930's and 1940's. I could not understand her desires to travel. Men always adored her. What I saw was a single parent trying to still live her life in some respect and raise me; she provided well for me. She worshiped me and gave me anything I may have needed. What she was trying to do is difficult in raising a man-child. Do not get me wrong, there are plenty of single family homes where the mother or grandparent have succeeded in seeing their progeny find rewards in life without a male figure. There are so many numbers where not having the presence of a male figure has caused harm and behaviors unspeakable. I needed a positive role model. All I received was criticism and abuse. I do realize there are those who have endured far worse than what I may have experienced, yet my plight is unique unto itself. I really needed someone to protect and guide me.

This is what I faulted my mother with. She spoiled me rotten and I never appreciated anything and all the ingredients brewed the monster I was to become. I blamed her for everything that happened to me. I manipulated her as much as I could with buying me anything I wanted. I made her feel bad by saying to her how much I did not care or love her. This in itself was heart wrenching to her, yet and still, she loved and worried about me. She purchased a home on her own and struggled each and every day working to provide. My mother gave birth to me at a late age – she was 43 years of age. This also bothered me because she started to suffer from arthritis and along came Parkinson Disease and it aged her even more. I disliked the fact people often took her for my grandmother. I resented having her attend any affair concerning me. My choice of words cut deep into her. I say to myself as a child, strange days of springtime introduced its soothing breezes upon the virtuousness of my heart.

As a youngster I welcomed the moment as I sat in the corner somewhere drifting towards serenity. As a kid I had escaped the inevitable once again and remained hidden so pressure could leave me for a while. Natives (my mother's friends), were trying to imprison me into some sort of diabolical way of abuse. They searched for me as always. I had to always have a venue of relief before I would have to carry my load of everlasting pain. As a child my days of freedom were minimal and my time was spent in reclusive fear. I was afraid of what I faced through those eyes as an innocent child, I felt alone and my tears went unanswered which I accused my mother of not being there to protect me.

I often wished death would not only come for me, but my Mom as well. I thought she was weak. She allowed people to have their way too much. I never looked at the virtue in kindness God had given her. All I thought of was how she allowed individuals to dictate her life. I can now see the self-hatred I was beginning to have was all because of being assaulted. You see, I can now piece together the events as to why I turned to a life of detriment and despair. I can see how I pitied myself and continued to give myself transfusions of pain. I still question where do we begin to change our lives and become renewed? How much effort must it take to revise our perspectives away from the selfishness and thoughtlessness we once permitted to prescribe our lives? I cried many days and was suicidal all because I did not understand the feelings I was enduring. This whisper of disapproval always instructed me to end it all. I thought everyone would be glad I was gone. I knew it would kill my mother and that was fine with me. I also did little needling things to disrupt her days. Deliberately making her miss the bus or just doing something to hurt her feelings.

I never physically hit my mother, but some of the wayward ways I was being treated sexually, started to construct another suit of perversion onto me. All young boys experiment with learned behavior. We think it is ok to do to others what has been done to us. I was no different. Because of my mistreatment, I was always willing and looking for those to try what I learned thinking it was ok. Whenever my mother would drag me along to her friend's house as a youngster, I would be set-up in a room to watch TV while they drank and had their fun. My mother's friends were all old, as I saw it like her, so they would sit around as I mentioned and retrace their memories. I would immediately go through their belongings looking for what to steal or to touch and feel their bras and panties.

Masturbation started early for me because of what I saw and participated in with the monsters who allowed me to touch and fondle them. Learned behavior can be a hardship and calamity; especially when all you see and feel is filth and the flesh is weak, as all the good books say. Touching in places of arousal can be just as potent as a drug. Temporary relief just like drugs; causing blockage of whatever painful situation that may arise. That is why today you see so many out of wedlock children in my opinion. Two young individuals frustrated because of economics and at home decide to relieve themselves with sex, which alleviates whatever they may be going through. A quick fix and in the end another unwanted child arrives and the cycle of ignorance continues.

So I would just begin to emulate what I saw and engaged in. I even found myself fondling my mother when she was asleep. I always tried to sneak a look as all boys do I guess. My mother tolerated me and did her best to give what I needed to survive. I wanted to kill those who I thought took advantage of her. I guess you can say it was a love-hate relationship. I never really had the opportunity to engage my father as I wanted to. Early on when I was a little boy, my smiles and happiness was there when I saw him. I think his absence and having predators hunt and have me as they chose, changed my perception of my relationship with him. I became fearful of people, including my father because of the trauma being put into me by an individual.

It is like not wanting to be close after being stung by just about everything. We become reluctant and hesitant. Over the years he and I were cordial. He found out in 1968 that I was involved with drugs and he tried to save me; but I had made up my mind that you cannot tell me what to do – and this is why trying to put corrections on young people's lives after missing the formative years is difficult. The early years are so crucial and if you miss out on putting your signature in a child's life then, too much time has elapsed to amend the situation. It was extremely challenging because I was just about the only kid at that time without the presence of a man each and every day in my home. I saw many men periodically come through to see my mother, but they were like nomads stopping by our home; the oasis for drinks and laughter. It all made no sense to me.

Darkness

Night-time sessions so horrible they can be. No daylight for hours what a scary thing that can be. When sounds of the night make you fear and wish for light – there may come to you a shape for real. To strip you bare while you stare and try to stay wake before it's too late. Now I tell you what darkness can be – such miserable moments placed upon your heart.

Fear and Becoming Mentally Ill

Sometimes our spirits are broken, shattered and scattered across the plains of no resolutions. I myself have been subjected to difficulty at times as it intertwined itself into my heart. During these periods of unrest, I found myself questioning life and wishing for a way to escape. In my reprieve from these moments I only found refuge in broken promises, which I have made to myself. I became a procrastinator of fear. It held me prisoner throughout my life; dictating my every move as a jailer. In a darkened room where fear enslaved me; I sat quietly, not wanting to add to my anguish.

Growing up with these attachments has turned my life into a horror. I have wished for death because I could not understand why. I searched the heavens for answers and have been ambivalent to my place in this world. I cried and been a victim of my own self-destruction. I have been heartache for those who have tried to love me. I just did not know what to do sometimes. My life has come a long way and I have adapted. I spend more time being happy now than before, but there are moments when I feel like those slaves who were brought here and had their spirits broken. They have moved on, but you never forget the day when you were broken, when your spirit left you, and all that was left was a corner in the dark with only stillness as your companion.

I could feel myself becoming more depressed early on. I wore a mask and was deceptive. It is difficult to explain how unbalanced I was becoming. I believe when people are traumatized it is like a seed implanted that is chronic and you do not even realize your suffering from being spoiled, blotted, or even slowly destroyed within.

According to research, antisocial personality disorders is a type of chronic mental illness in which a person's ways of thinking, perceiving situations and relating to others are abnormal and destructive. People with antisocial personality disorders typically have no regard for right and wrong. They may often violate the law and the rights of others, landing in frequent trouble or conflict. They may lie, behave violently, and have drug and alcohol problems. People with antisocial personality disorders may not be able to fulfill responsibilities to family, work or school. Antisocial personality disorder is sometimes known as sociopathic personality disorder. A sociopath is a particularly severe form of antisocial personality disorder. Now this defines me at one time in my life. Each description of this kind of behavior was my life. There were moments when my actions were defiant, difficult and eventually perverse with a lot of issues and circumstances. My downward spiral was slow and yet the filthiness I felt for myself was overwhelming. The fear controlled any moment towards trying to correct my nature. A lot of us are handcuffed through fear. I was afraid to tell what had been done to me and that left me fearful of many other segments of my life. I was afraid of relationships. The biggest reason was the phobias and inadequacies I felt.

My insecurities were many and worsened over periods of time. I did not trust myself, let alone others. Being tall and lanky added to the lack of confidence I had in myself. I had this Walter Mitty mindset whereas I dreamed of being everything but myself. I took on identities from all sorts of characters. I was always afraid of how people perceived me. I was always concerned that people could see the filth on me. How troubling life can be when you are scrambled and mixed-up. I was becoming destructive to myself and others. I thought engaging in wrongful acts was the right thing to do. I violated myself and others and committed some criminal activities I had never been prosecuted for.

Nothing was ordinary with me – and what is strange is how I masked much of what I was experiencing until I began to burst inside. I always contemplated suicide. I was fascinated with the thought of ending it all. I felt as though if I died I would not have to endure the suffering I felt inside. I did not have the heart or courage to cut my wrist. I guess that is why I took a slow course in suicide through drugs. Why I acted the way I did, and allowed myself to repeat the same scenarios over and over again. Why I had no regard at times for my purpose and worthiness in life is without any doubt, because of my inability to recognize and to face my own idiosyncrasies. Those handicapped measures I carried through life by choice are behavior patterns I permitted to define my inconsideration, thoughtlessness, and don't give a damn perspective. Being mentally ill I could never have accepted back then because in my mind I thought my problems stemmed from those I hated.

Bare

Naked as a winter tree I am. This is about me, why should you really care? I want relief from despair. Provocateurs invade my mind. They bring a bag, full of the past. I combat it with spilling my guts; you see, I'm working on me. Bare as you can see the nightmare began, encoded within, decipher this menace I must. I have time. Pealing this bark away to discover the real me. Unless you know who I am?

Confusion

In high school I continued to spiral out of control. Things were unraveling and I became more and more delusional. My cowardice as a human being was evident as I took all measures to never become anything but a drug addict and bum. It was a slow process. I was depriving myself of what I could have become. I took every measure to fail. I made sure I did nothing to achieve. I dug my hole in the ground of my existence each and every day of my life back then. I became accustomed to being labeled a failure or someone involved with the drug life. Having meaningless conversation was the hip thing to do.

Most of us have experienced this fantasy world, but trauma was a reality for me. I took pride in being associated with those considered dangerous or a role model. I can remember being in situations which were compelling and stupid. I wanted on many occasions to walk away, but I was always worrying about not being accepted. That was such an issue with me. I have no doubt that I was a people pleaser, as they say. I used to give anything to be liked. I looked for love and care in all the wrong places. I even got to the point of puncturing my arms and losing my mental health.

When I was alone I was in so much pain that I did not understand why. Why, was always foreign and never gave me an inclination as to which direction I should go. I had no religious foundation which may have gotten me on some sort of straight and narrow. I just had a bad relationship with God. I always asked why He let me be abused and become the monster I was becoming. I felt there was no such thing as a loving God. If so, then why was the world and me in so much chaos and pain? Why was darkness a part of my existence? And why did I not have two loving parents together, taking me to be cultured and protecting me? I always wondered why my parents, though not together, never wanted to participate in any events concerning me. I always felt embarrassed about my mother because of her age. My father was just not there and I had to deal with the hand I had. I was always in the picture frame with my selfishness, bad attitude, and ego. No wonder I could not see the picture. I was in the damn frame. Everything had to be about me.

I can recall early on each and every time my mother took me to get a haircut on Amherst Street in East Orange, New Jersey. I can still see the barbers and how accompanying they were to my mother. I used to hate the fact they looked at her in a certain way. I felt awkward as hell with her sitting in there with me. I guess in some respect this added to my disappointments within myself. It was these moments and the sessions in abuse that caused me to start to look at the world in many ways. More negative than positive. Having a father may have saved me even though my dislike for him was evident. I hated myself for being fearful of, and disappointed in him. My mother did everything for me. He was never around to do the things that kids need fathers for. My anguish with myself and those around me became even more puzzling. I was a confused person.

My gravitating towards drugs more and more appeased my pain. I always found a way to put myself in the dark, always found the right moments to come-up short in one way or another. I was shooting drugs; I had made it to my own mountaintop. The progression was slowly happening as I wandered amongst the walking dead. I was still functional, yet my belief system was shattered and I became like many of us today; lying claim to victimhood.

I knew everyone in the Oranges back then. I was still able to function and loved getting high and playing basketball. I never reached my potential athletically because I was walking on the wild side. I never put the effort that is needed to become successful. I do believe if I had the focus one needs to play sports or do anything, I would have succeeded. I never had anyone to really push me back then. Everyone always had some negative shit to say about me. I cannot blame them as I look at it now because I was giving the people what they were talking about concerning me. Yes, I mistreated my mother which was talked about; yes I did not care, and of course I had no rules I truly lived by. In my own madness I thought people were mistreating me. That was the depth of my illness and addiction. I could play ball and established a name for myself. I was a street ballplayer like so many who had a good game, but I loved to be in darkness. I say the darkness because there was something about being negative that may seem hard for some to understand. Call it peer pressure or low self-esteem; it was thrilling to do messed up stuff. I guess when you do not know yourself you are bound to take on identities you think are who you are; but in reality it is all in your imagination and the wanting to be other than your natural self. It is like living beyond your means, knowing you cannot afford things, but spending anyway to be a part of something or present a certain image. Now that's insanity!

We played at the Valley Settlement House. When I first started going there, it was more whites attending than Blacks. It was on the borderline of West Orange and Orange. Once more of us started to attend; the white population decreased. That is the way it was in most areas at one time populated by whites. When Blacks started moving in, white flight became a reality. Even on my street there were Irish, Italian, Polish all living with no problems. Then the exodus came and all that changed, this and other events became the end to an integration of civility. In my life change always seemed damaging.

There were moments when there was no clear understanding what life meant for me. I had no idea what being normal meant or what it was supposed to look like; and it is difficult because when you are framed along the lines of a kid with issues and those so-called issues are reinforced through constant mistreatment to some degree, depression and other mental instability measures start to take its place. I just really never gave thinking of myself inside as nothing but a piece of shit. I thought I was worthless and being made to feel damaged increases this kind of thought process. I just wandered along with shores of fear on my feet avoiding pain by medicating myself by all things to decease the pain. I look at that time and how my life was troubled. There were many times even after I had gotten older, that a lack in emotional growth showed itself in my life. I just drifted along never truly investing to better myself.

I had found the answer to my sorrow and pain with drugs; and took pride in having a track to develop on my arm. I took issue with making sure I scratched just as much as everyone else. It's like a foolish competition of an individual's self-destructive behavior. At times, I found myself constantly available for money from those who had abused me. I never thought that my life was heading the wrong way. I guess I wanted to die or to just drift off somewhere to parts unknown. I now can see how I had prostituted myself. When I thought about writing my life story, I wanted at first to pick and choose what I wanted read about me. A part of me cared what people may think. Then I said to myself, *'Does it really make a difference? Should I really care about how the world perceives me at this stage of my life?'* This is what contributed to my failures in the first place. I did not want to window-dress my life as though I would mention this and keep this secret. Your secrets can do more harm than desired.

When I look over the facts of my life I can honestly say I prostituted myself many times in numerous situations. It is not always sexually, but there are many ways to sell one's self. There were times when I was sick and made myself available to engage in all sorts of perverted behavior. Being stroked at such a young age, you become a part of murky behavior. What is usually done to you stays a snapshot in your memories and the flesh is weak, as they say. There were circumstances with my jailers when it was not painful or shameful. I also started to take pleasure in being taken to perimeters of climaxing. I can only speak of what was done to me or what actions I participated in. I had to make sure when starting to pen this that the shame and guilt that followed most of these acts had been put into its rightful place; long ago.

It still is a process when yesterday comes and visits. I understand how my own equations became entangled where no resolution was enacted to avoid the destruction I did to my life. How befuddling times were when emptiness always seemed to be the monologue of my existence. I can recall being baited because the need to get money at times became a demand in my life. I stole when I could, but jail always alarmed me. So I was a sneak as they say. Doing just enough to stay under the radar and drowning in my own madness with little attention as I could. There are many out there who more than likely did whatever it took to get what they needed as well. I can recall many times being picked-up while walking home. I could not care less nor considered it may have been a mass murderer. I just did what had to do to get what I wanted.

I never was on the receiving end of any situations. Nevertheless, I engaged both male and female individuals. There can be no exemptions to this story for the sake of family, friends, or anyone who does not know my background. I decided to get buck naked and let the truth hit where it may. I may get strange reactions or even suspected in some strange way, but reality is, I have to acknowledge what was done to me, what irrelevancy surrounded my life and bear my cross for others to know that I too, have been down a road where carelessness and disregard for myself was a part of my existence. I sometimes cry even today when I think about the blessing in me after all that I have been through. I could be sick from the arenas I played in or be jailed for years with no release in sight, or I could be a murderer or anything where madness lurks because of trauma.

Some have asked whether I feel ashamed of what I did or whether I understand why. I have no answer as to why my creator allowed me to cope with what I have endured. There are many who have been through more than me. There are those still living with the trauma that still inflicts and dictates their lives. I always knew the difference between right and wrong. I just chose to walk on the wild side because of the sickness in the thoughts I carried. I thought I was worthless and much of the times I wore this face of contentment, I was always disturbed, unstapled, and unhinged. I never wanted more than the crumbs of life. I never sought anything but self-destruction. As much as one may think today of what they see in me, it has always been the way it is. I can honestly state that immorality, rudeness, and filthiness had once been my personality. The illness always showed itself in many facets in my life. I truly believed that my unhappiness was my fault. It never dawned on me that what I may have been going through was part of my illness developing. I was consistently fearful of just about everything. I was afraid of just waking up and facing my life as a child. I was afraid of how others saw me. Even at a young age, I was intimidated about everything. Even though there are many chains of events that happened and were constantly reinforced and recreated, my mental illness had adopted me. I embraced it and just existed.

Bette

I was in high school when I met my former wife, Bette. I had heard of her and really respected her brother's basketball game. He had graduated by the time I got to high school but I used to go see him play with Dino who also graduated with him. I heard so much about Bette and her beautiful voice. She was a singer. All of us thought in our hearts and souls that we were singers back then. Even I thought I was the next lead singer of a group of guys who met at my house to howl like cats. But Bette was truly a professional.

I started speaking with her sister before Bette but life changed that and we began a relationship in 1969. She had just cut her first record which the whole town of Orange was excited about. She lived crosstown where the projects were and each section of Orange had its differences and different status. You had people who lived in the 7 Oaks section who were upper-middle class African-Americans, and the Valley people living below the railroad tracks and people from crosstown. Each area had certain feelings and attitudes about the other real tribalism. I always had feelings about people from that area because coming up it was always a feeling you had to be ready to fight. All the so-called tough people came from the area.

Bette was joyful and had a great family. She had two sisters and two brothers, lovely parents and a father who did not take crap from anyone. Bette saw her grandmother and her great-grandmother. So when my own daughter was born like the other grandkids, they were seen and held by multiple legacies. Bette and I as young people, enjoyed our youth and doing the things young people engaged in. She was truly the first female in my age bracket I had sex with. It was something different and I guess this is why my love for her became intense and our love affair escalated. She had graduated before I did so my mother sought out her assistance to push me through school. I was still hanging out and doing my deviance whenever I could find the time.

Drugs were becoming an even bigger part of my life. As a matter a fact, there were a bunch of us at school whose thinking was identical to mine. We started shooting drugs right there in the bathrooms. As I look back now what a crime I committed on myself. What a tragedy and monstrosity I was becoming along with many others. Selling drugs and going to school not to learn but to destroy myself was my daily calling. I look back and have no idea how I made it through school and many other episodes in my life.

I had gotten kicked off the basketball team for being caught smoking reefer in the bathroom by the coach. News ran through the school about what happened and it took place when we were playing against our rival East Orange High School. It was an important game because of an ongoing matchup between me and their star player. I was in no shape mentally or physically to play against this guy. If I had been focused as he was I would have no doubt of my ability.

Bette continued to push me as she was going to have our child in 1972, along with about 12 other girls in the town. Both of her sisters were pregnant as well. I did not want this baby and I did everything but push her down the stairs to not have it. I began to tear her down emotionally whenever I could. In my ignorance, insanity and confusion, I did not want her to have the baby because it might inherit my traits. I thought so low of myself and that any child would be like me; a piece of shit. So I campaigned for her to not have the baby. I put those thoughts out there in the universe. Each time I could make her stressful and cry I would. I truly was mean and in the end, my wish became a reality. She had gone into labor on May 8, 1972, a Monday morning after having a baby shower that Sunday. I got word and my heart started to pump and a reflection of a baby who I did not want responsibility for and think it would be as confused as I was, shattered me. She stayed in the labor from that morning until the evening when they discovered the baby was dead inside her. Why it took over nine hours to figure this out is still a mystery. Nevertheless, my wishes came true and I breathed a sigh of relief. Inside I felt guilty as though I had personally aborted the baby. We both were saddened and when they said the baby looked like the father, a part of me felt remorse but another part of me felt like I am glad no child who looks like me and have my traits should be born. This is how insane my thinking was. We named him Brian and he was buried in Baby Land by her father and the healing for her began as I continued to spiral out of control.

Bette's younger sister had her baby the next week, and her older sister had her child that January. So out of all the girls who had babies, ours was a loss. She was depressed and I did my best to be there for her in some respect, but in reality I felt relieved. This is how uncomfortable I was with me. When I think about it my self-esteem and the way I saw me, was that of a fiend. Suicide was still an option and the thoughts always were there to just end it, and escape this thing called life. They inserted an IUD in Bette and did not want her to get pregnant right away; I was all for that. I graduated and made it through, how I have no idea. Bette was still there and I used to meet her either at lunch time or after work to get money to buy drugs.

I was drafted into the military and that was a short stint, after manipulating my mom to make a way to arrange to get me out because I was a sole surviving son. I came home and just started to cause havoc for my mother and everyone in my path. Bette got pregnant again with the IUD in her and they did not want to chance taking it out while the fetus was in the way of such a procedure, so she carried the baby. On March 28, 1974 my oldest child was born. Bette and I had gotten married while she was pregnant in 1974. The ceremony was performed at Union Baptist Church in Orange, New Jersey by the same preacher who christened me. Our daughter was a lovely for me. My mother adored her deeply. I accepted. She was a girl which made some perverted difference than a boy. We lived with my mother and I started working at Orange Memorial Hospital like most of the people in the town. We were basically being taken care of by my mother. We never had enough to pay bills because I was getting high and doing my crap.

I had entered rehab a couple of times, but it was no use. My first arrest for drugs came in 1974 while Bette was pregnant; the East Orange police arrested me at 40 Washington Street in East Orange, New Jersey. I was booked and my mother bailed me. I went before a judge and was put into Conditional Discharge Program. I had to go to meetings and probation and if I did not get into any more offenses this could be considered an expungement from my record. Well I got through not going to jail but there were a few more arrests.

During the late 70's, with a child between us, Bette started to do her thing. I cannot blame her now, although back then I thought she was being cruel. Can you imagine that after all the evil things I thought about doing to her, I came to the conclusion I was being mistreated! I never mentioned to my daughter when she got older anything about my antics, but they were known and I was labelled a loser. I never said anything of what Bette did to me because quite frankly, she had every right to.

Every weekend, Bette and her older sister would go out and not come home until the break of dawn. She used to leave my daughter with me and if I argued I was not going to keep her, she would put the baby on my Mom. I cannot say for sure what Bette was doing while out, but it would not surprise me if she was entertaining someone else. Sex had become masturbation every now and then, but drugs were Bette's biggest competitor. I was a little boy of nothingness with so many mental issues. She knew she had to exit, and who could blame her. I came home so high one day that when I woke, everything she could take was gone. She left me! I cried, not for the loss of my family, but because my enabler was gone. I had brought friends who were shooting drugs to live with us in our times of moving from here to there. I was losing jobs and started taking pills, heroin, and drinking; everything I could get my hands on to get high. Bette did the best thing by exiting, which any woman should do when faced with such madness.

Bette still would bring our daughter to my mother's where I lived. I started going to my cousin's in New York all the time as a place of refuge. One particular time I had my daughter when she was four years old, we went to see *The Wiz* movie. I was high and decided during the movie to go outside and leave her there to get some more drugs if I could find it. I was gone about 20 minutes, and we all know it takes no time to kidnap a kid. I did not consider the severity of my actions because everything was about destroying me. I believe when someone is in the process of killing himself, they affect everything around them. I was always endangering my child. I even took her to an area in Newark called Pill Hill to buy narcotics.

Bette met someone and my behavior was well known, so he protected her from me as I became a wanderer of life. I was drifting from here and there. I was riding the Path train to my cousins and sleeping in Penn Station at times. My Mom was now living in a senior Citizen complex and could not have me there, but I stayed and hid whenever I could. Bette and I had nothing more to do with one another except our child. I must confess and thank her for the many times she tolerated loving me the way she did. Most people loved me, but I always thought the worst of me did not deserve to be loved. I also want to say to her, *'Thank you for being a friend.'* To our daughter with whom I have had a very estranged relationship, *'I love you and I am sorry I was not there to hold and protect you, and be the father you wanted. Your mother did the best thing in escaping my madness. She gave you a chance to live away from someone like me; a lost and troubled individual.'*

Nightmares

There were years wasted where my survival was tested each and every day. These are the times I twisted more and more. I was being hospitalized for all the reasons we get when living dangerously. People around me were dying and I was waiting for my turn. Depression was always upon my shoulders because I saw nothing which could stabilize my life. I was killing my mother emotionally and my Aunt Mae, who lived with her, I began to mistreat as well. I had been in and out of the VA Hospital in East Orange, New Jersey. I was finally convinced to go to a long term program in Montrose, New York. I went to Franklyn Delano Roosevelt Psychiatric Hospital. The building where I was housed was for substance abusers which in reality, was a place where people with thinking problems were housed. This therapeutic environment was supposed to help but it was just another place to waste valuable years of my life. I too believe the spirit directs us to places where we can feel safe and sort things out. I say that because if I would have gotten what I truly deserved, I would have died years ago.

I was out of it in that facility and was painting rocks down by the Hudson River for fifty cents a day. I had arts and crafts like a kid. Everywhere we went we had to go as a group or with another person. I painted the woodshop a bright yellow and orange because they were trying to change the color scheme from institutional grey. The groups were always trying to trigger people's thinking. Eventually I would take over the house and would be giving directives using therapeutic lingo and playing this game, never truly serious about changing. I would drink when I came home on furlough and so I was still finding a way to abuse me. My Mom was getting sick and older and she was happy I was away somewhere. She always worried what would happen to me if she died. She knew people thought I could not stand on my own two feet if something happened to her. On my visits home I would occasionally see my daughter before going back upstate to the hospital. Upon returning, you were tested for drugs but not alcohol.

I still had issues about why I thought of myself as inadequate. Besides Bette, women my Mom's age were what I was accustomed to. My thinking about sex was still handicapped because of my self-esteem, and always questioning my strange thoughts. I was still harboring what was done to me and allowing it to keep me thinking guilty. I felt ashamed of my experience as a child and how I had grown into being a vessel for others to inflict there predatory symptoms into me. I always questioned why I just went along with things as though this is the norm. The questions of why, became my thought, *'I must be like them.'* Filthy and a horror I was.

During one of my train rides back to the hospital I met a guy who had a rooming house in White Plains, New York. After getting a factory job in Elmsford, New York, I left the hospital and moved into the rooming house. When I moved in, my rent was $40.00 a week. I knew the guy was gay and I also knew he probably rented the room to get me into his rooming house. I was catching the bus to the job which paid $110.00 per week so I could pay rent and survive. I would still catch the train to Harlem every weekend. My landlord also went into the City to wherever he hung out on weekends. Around this time, I started taking pills again. I would go to New Jersey or 116th Street in Harlem to what was described as a 30; USV (SEBER) pills with codeine. Also at this time, I received notice of settlement for $10,000.00 in a car accident case where my arm had been broken. I went through the first increment check of $2,500.00 quickly. I bought a fur coat from Alexander's in New York and I got everyone high. When you have something to give, no matter what it is, you have friends. Once you are on empty everyone disappears. I began to have a relationship with my landlord – because of the early abuses from predators, I still thought that this was what I was supposed to do when I needed to survive.

Money was gone and once again I had created something in my life to keep me from finding who I am. I was confused and the behavior of prostituting me in some way was all I thought myself worth. I never thought I was gay or nothing, I just thought I was a worthless abomination and disgrace; and because of believing I was good for nothing, my mind kept spinning like a top. This is wrong inside for me. I am not being biased against those who live that lifestyle and I am not one to judge. I just know from me, we have choices and what I was engaging in was not because of a belief of any sort, it was because of early on things done to me; of being so beat down about me. I was living a life of thinking this is all I was worth.

The decisions I made at those times are what kept me chasing death; kept my nightmares coming. I was standing in pools of shame and because of that, I participated in anything that was deemed wrong to add to my abnormal thinking. I have forgiven myself as part of my healing; it is not beating me up because of what I did. It is what I had become as a result of what I had been through. Regardless as to how others may interpret this, I could not care less – what I did at one time as I sneaked through the shadows of life, doing my doings, and hoping what I did stayed in the dark. I lived on the cracks of life always hiding in some way as the cloak of my shame held me captive. My experience in selling me, is a bygone of what becomes of the brokenhearted who does not love himself. I hated me, so I added more and more shame onto me. I wanted to make things clear because at times in my life I would give so much of me, which allowed me to remain frozen in darkness. I was living in the dark.

This was just another experience of what I used to be. I made it personal in my life. Sometimes when we personalize circumstances, we add unhappiness to us. I am not gay by any means, I was just a participator in experiences I thought I did not care one way or another about at that time. I was crap any way I looked at it. I am not the only one out there who has done things in the dark they choose to keep hidden. People of all walks of life have done something questionable they would prefer to keep hidden. If they say they do not, they are liars with no truth in them. I had scars which were bleeding every day of my life back then. The dark was my comforter and that is all it was. I choose to live in the light today, what I did is behind me. *"Let he who is without sin cast the first stone."* John 8:7.

Prior to going to Montrose, New York for rehabilitation, I worked for the US Postal Service at their facility in Kearney, New Jersey. I was fired because of my drug use. I found out that I could possibly get my job back since I had completed a program. So I cleaned up, got my job back, and started to move forward. The problem was, I had still not dealt with mental me. I started dating a girl at the job and once again, my dark shadow lifestyle was in full effect. Even though I was drug free, my thinking and behavior had not changed. My heart was still corrupt. She was helping me to adjust. We moved into an apartment, and eventually bought a home together. This was the usual me; selling myself at all cost to get what I needed. I bought a new Honda Accord, was clean and sober, and gained weight. I dressed up the outside of me, but never the inside pain I had flowing throughout my nature.

Soon I got involved with another woman, a cashier at the post office who was seven years younger and built like a brick house. I liked this woman a lot. We both had issues for sure. She and I were both labelled. Out of everyone in the post office, I got the prize. She was fascinating! My penis came back to life and now I am living with one woman and beginning a romance with another. I got a credit card and I flew her and myself to see my family in the Bahamas. She made me feel something I had not felt in a long time; sexually alive. I managed to embarrass her and myself and the woman I lived and bought a home with. I lied and said I was going to the Bahamas alone, but the young girl went with me.

Again I caused a bad situation just like I did when I got busted smoking reefer in high school; when I got busted with the little girl upstairs from me, and now this circumstance. Everyone in the post office knew what I did. Because of my disrespect for others, I became the object of everyone's disgust and conversation. Arguments ensued and I started using again. The relationship ended as I began to unravel, piece-by-piece. I was driving while drugged-up and crashed my car. The girl I lived with, she and I both started running on the railroad tracks of drug addiction. I also took her to the Bahamas to make-up with my daughter and hers. This woman and I spent more money on drugs and the girl I was seeing faded away.

I must tell this though; while teaching a college class years later, she came up to me and said, *"Earl?'* I was startled – did not know what to say and dismissed her in a flash. I said *'Hello and excuse me.'* I had to go sort through seeing her again. The next time I saw her, I apologized and we talked. I found out she had her own addiction issues to come to terms with and was married. She seemed like me, at peace. I was a health professor when she took my class and it was difficult to talk about the sexual part of health knowing she had been with me sexually and knows me unclothed. I was uncomfortable. But that is what life does; puts us in uncomfortable situations to grow and develop us. *'Thank you'* to her for helping make complete that part of my life with her that needed closing. God bless her. I lost my job at the Post Office. The girl I had bought the house with moved into the other side of our duplex and started a relationship with someone incarcerated. The other young lady drifted away. We all had used every nickel and dime we had to buy drugs.

My mother was now in White House Nursing Home in Orange, New Jersey. Usually when I went to see her it was to beg for money out of her account; always lying about this or that. I would roll her down to the window to get money, but if she needed help to the bathroom, I was too selfish to help her. This woman who birthed me, helped me when I was helpless, saw me with needles in my arm and struggled with me; I did not even help to the toilet. I was regressing back to that guy with the suit of pain.

I was working for the City of Newark, New Jersey when my Mom died on March 8, 1986. I thought I would join her because that was what was said out of the mouths of those who knew how awful I treated her. I was so distraught and drugged up that I could not get out of the hearse at the gravesite. I did not want to see her lowered into the ground without me going with her. When Little Mama died, that was a nightmare, but I managed to carry my Mom to New York for the funeral. The night after we buried my mother, brought another tragedy. A dear former co-worker at the Post Office had been shot by her husband after just leaving my house. Everyone was devastated! We were summoned to trial and made to relive that nightmare. I needed to get away. I was on a serious cocaine and pill chase. My arms were sore from sticking myself and I was paranoid.

I was so beaten and my physical body was beginning to turn on me. I needed to find God and ask Him why he had let me endure this suffering and emptiness. My whole life up to that point was a nightmare; a life of void and never loving me. All I thought about was how the end would come. The darkness I was in led me down so many roads of chaos. The drugs, the bad people, like myself, who never gave themselves a chance. The danger I saw and crimes I committed; not only against others, but myself. I had once beaten a guy with a stick, knocking pieces of his ear off. It was all over money I wanted. Sometimes I wanted to walk away but was kept in place because I did not want to look like a punk. I was a coward but did not want to look like one. I did not have the heart to do some of things I did and was around, but I was immobile and refusing to move. The many times cursing God and hating the very thing He created me. I had overdosed and He awakened me and I cursed why did He not let me just die. My tears and anguish was vast. The shame and guilt I keep mentioning, had me so full of hopelessness that I did not care. I thought about how the monsters and had come to my room. I thought about screaming, afraid of what may come in the dark. I thought about looking down into my casket smiling. I had finally gotten it done. I reflected on all the moments which if He did not have His hand on me, I would be gone.

There was a time on Branford Place in an alley we called Neutral Alley, where I cannot account of how I got there, I blacked out and from 11:00am until 4:00am the next morning. I do not know what happened back there but I had a wound on my left hip. All I knew was I could not walk and had to crawl out that alley and flag down a car to call for an ambulance. He had His hand on me when I got hit in the face with a bat of sort in a crap game and was found wandering with my face in my hands on Central Avenue in need of minor plastic surgery. These are some of the things I thought about as my life was spared again by the Orange Police Department when they arrested me. This piece to my puzzle was the beginning of my beginning. Never did I realize God had a plan for me. He had always been there, but it was I who had forgotten me.

Cubicle of Despair

I chose to sit in the square by the door entrance. I was afraid, as I sat still as I could, not making a sound, not wanting to be found. This cubicle is a comfort zone of sort, it's the last place they would look. Waiting to hear a key in the lock so I could embrace freedom for the moment it came up. In this space I never moved, just sat there in place blinking not once. Breathing softly with my tiny heart beating. My despair was beside me punching my soul. Escape is on my other side inching me on. The decision to move could be rather costly. For the predators could capture me. Something I could not stand. Question marks before my eyes, do I break? Or do I stay in my cubicle of despair? I ran!

CHAPTER 4
THE ROAD TO DAMASCAS

The Mountaintop

I was finished. It was time for the mending to begin. I was beaten for sure and my life was slipping away. I suffered because of choice and it was always comfortable to blame others for my pain. Here I was having lost precious years of my life, banged-up and sick from one thing or another. I broke so many bones except my leg, neck, and foot. My inside turmoil was eroding. I had piled years of trauma – one atop of the other. It was always the same shame of being abused, engaging in selling myself, guilty by being alive, and just being unclear about why I am here, living each and every day. I saw no purpose for me, and I came to believe what was said about me, over and over again – *"I am not shit, never going to be shit."*

I wore the crown fashioned for me. Every time I stuck a needle in my arm or swallowed pills I went with the intention of killing me. I deserved death, I thought, because so many had said I was not even shit. The same people who judged me, who verbally beat me down were the one's adding to my demise early on by inflicting the hatred they had for themselves into me. I needed to hate me and I was a candidate for this arena of guilt and shame for sure. After all, I was a kid who mistreated his mother, never listened to anyone and who they said needed his ass beat. I was the kid who each and every day before I went to my own mountain top hated his very existence. I was the kid who when no one was looking was being molested, injured emotionally, and tormented until I went to my own mountain top. I grew in disgust for life. Why was I here? What is the reason this creature of loathe spared? What could anyone possibly strain from me? I hated God, people and me. I had missed so much good in life. I was disappointing as a father, husband, son and friend. No one knew until almost my end, why I never screamed or told what was happening to me on so many nights and even days. Never did I realize God had a plan for me that would be found on a mountain in Pennsylvania; there I would begin to find what was missing from my life. It is always through what we cannot fathom or understand, that moves God to come and set the record straight.

I left for the mountain on New Year's Eve 1988 or 1989. It is these times of admittance that are dangerous for addicts. They convinced me to meet them on Springfield Avenue in Irvington at McDonald's. I did not know this ride would transform me and I would come to know my Lord. All through the ride there were questions and answers and I was being an ass like I know it all. I was good at the recovery lingo. We arrived safely to the mountain and the rehabilitation placed named White Deer. Never did I know such spiritual things would take place in my life. I went in there talking the usual but there was something different happening. The groups seemed all about me and that made me afraid. I was keeping everyone sick, as they say, because I had experience in challenging and arguing what is not important. One day a guy showed up to group. This man was strange because he did not seem like he fit the mold of someone with an addiction problem and he never said anything. He just periodically looked at me and I would give a *'do you know me?'* kind of return stare.

White Deer was very foreign and strange. It was unlike any rehab I had ever been to. It appeared as though the people who ran my cottage winked their right eye; strange! They would constantly say to me privately, *"When are you going to talk about it?"* 'Talk about what?' I thought. Now that was foreign! No one had ever asked me to talk about IT. I was told that only one or two would make it out of there whole because they had chosen to do the right thing; tell.

In the pit of my soul, something was starting to boil. During some group sessions they would mention things that triggered something inside of me. I went to see the minister there and he winked his eye as well. He said to me, *"You will live."* I thought to myself, *'Why would he say that?'* Something was happening to me. One night I and knelt cried as I looked into the heavens and knew I was beginning to give up those secret tapes we all have. I thought to myself that whenever I was away and saw people flip out because of pain, that was something I would never do. I made a decision – I would never tell my past. I was going to my grave with all the shame, guilt and other sticky issues I thought were too embarrassing and terrible.

That very night I went to see a counselor and quietly started to take him through my life. I wept and wept as he made me confess to all that I was ashamed of. All the guilt trailed behind the shame. It was as though I was with a priest having confession. He held me at times when it became so overwhelming. I felt faint and he did not let me fall. He said, *"Finish it."* I finished and felt relieved until he said, *"If you really want to get better, you have to tell it out there in front of everyone."* He said, *"You have tell it in front of that mountain. Carry this cross you bear and nail you on this mountain for all to see and hear."* I immediately said, 'No. I will not expose myself out there.' *"If you want to live, you must do it,"* he said. The night was hard. I could not sleep thinking about doing what he said I must do. I was thinking no one else could have possibly been through what I have.

The next day the group started and that guy who I mentioned that had looked at me, seemed to be staring and I could feel something emanating from him. They were discussing something and I was on the edge of my seat, I could feel the boiling inside. I started to regurgitate and the guy looked even more into me. I stood up and threw out of me something demonic and painful. I shook all over and I was told I hit the floor and screamed. That little boy named me screamed! The little boy who was raped screamed! The times I sold me, was hurting, and all other moments, screamed! I was struggling and trying to clear what was coming out and it too, was pulling to stay in me. I screamed what I should have always screamed, the loss of my Mom and most of all my innocence. I laid there crumbled and when it was over I had come to find God.

I changed colors it seemed and I was at peace of some sort. I had just had an emotional surgery and I could not stop writing about God. The man I mentioned, the strange guy who stared; disappeared. Before he left, he also said, *"You will live."* As fast as he had come, he was gone. Although this moment is still imprinted into my life, it was an epiphany for me. I had left the pain, shame and guilt on that mountain and now I was ready to reinvent me. Now was time to continue to peel back and discover me and my purpose in life. God spared me for a reason and now I left all that had me chained, and walked away. I felt somewhat like Paul on his road to Damascus with an awakening to God.

On My Damascus Road

We all have these roads we travel down when our lives become perplexed and misunderstood. Our perceptions of reality are befuddled and we search for our purpose out of desperation. I myself was on such a road when my surroundings started to become unfamiliar and truth introduced itself, extending its majestic. I was at a point in my life where I was about to give up because despair had placed itself upon my shoulders. On this road a whisper from somewhere came, massaging my heart with a cascade of grace from which I started to weep. As my eyes closed and opened, a reflection of my inner self appeared and for once in my life I felt at peace. All my life I have been in pain of some sort. My crimes, shame, and guilt had taken its toll on this wretched individual I had become. My ego was my enemy because I had edged God out of my life for so long. He was always there but I chose to accept the invitation of iniquity and its wickedness. On my road it became apparent I could be forgiven. I am not an outcast. My soul reassured me that God loves me. A bad child I had become and yet paradise was still achievable for me. On this road everything became clear about me. I saw death with its hand extended and I saw life with open arms. Never in my life had I felt so serene.

The things which troubled my heart seemed a pastime – a mere insignificant. My body started to feel like a cloud floating along in harmony with the world. I realized I was being altered from what I was, back into the bosom of mercy. The leniency I have been afforded is a blessing. On this road, I have made peace with all of the scenarios which kept me captive for so long. On this road, I saw the sky and the gates of heaven as every moment of my life flashed before me. I was okay! I am not afraid anymore! My nakedness was stripping me of all those vices this world lured me into; the lewdness, immorality and dishonor. On this road to my Damascus, doubt was nowhere to be found. I have a new beginning. As I turned to begin my walk, there before my eyes were my sins and the person I used to be. I continued to stroll and never gave what was left there on that road a second thought. Compassion embraced me and together we walked into a pristine air of contentment. God had brought me home.

Derailed

There comes a time when virtue allows you to overcome the obstacles of yesterday's perturbing ways. How well informed I was of the hour which crept by slowly allowing me to observe how insignificant I am. My eyes see unbelievable terror, which seem to frighten my days on occasions. There have been so many results that are not very friendly to me. I question the sanity of this world in its counter ways of portraying stability. How long will my words linger along the road where I am the only one to capture the true essence of what is reliable for this explorer to comprehend? There becomes an opening for suggestions if one needs validity to sanction the reality of this thing we call life. I am along the tracks, walking carefully avoiding the power lines of distraction step by step. I creep trying to keep from running into myself. I only stop to cry and exhale my frustrations with tears, making a pool for me to weep and see a reflection of my sorrow. The journey becomes a pitiful experience at times, for I notice those who desire me to trip and fall. The struggle is a blessing in disguise at times. For I am a vase, who has a crack and has been mended by determination of forgiveness. The station before my way is a constellation of humiliation, a pit stop to recover from my evil ways. I must push forward – surrender to the illuminating reasons of why we all struggle thru hardship only to be rescued by ease as it throws its net of survival and love for this soldier who sometimes gets derailed along the tracks of this revelation we call life.

Walking in the Light

Even though I had this miraculous moment, there was still a mess I had created which I had to face. The bills I made, the heartbreaks I brought about and the rest of the catastrophe. The journey was about to begin in the light. All my life I traveled in darkness afraid of the light and what it meant. I just knew staying in darkness gave me irresponsibility and a host of other disasters to hold onto. Being wounded like we all may become at times, healing is a process and now it was time for me to learn to forgive myself and grow.

I came back to legal issues still after being found guilty on all four counts of drug disposition and possessions. I was facing 15 years but received 364 days in the county jail. I was permitted to do this time on the weekend and once again God was with me. I had a probation officer who came by the house to check on me. I was fined as well. He would take urine samples and I was on my way to resurrecting me. The woman I used to live with was right next door. She married this huge guy and started to try and provoke me into a confrontation. She was angry and tried to do everything to stop what God was making a way for. I started attending NA meetings and got a sponsor. I listened to others in the meetings who were talking about similar issues that I was facing. It was strange going to parties sober. I was afraid. Everything I did before my experience at White Deer, I had to be high. I could not participate unless I was on something to give me false courage. This newly found freedom allowed me to listen and learn from those others who had an identical past as I.

I made meetings and was employed by the City of Newark as a trash collector. I was evolving and the one thing that started to become fascinating was seeing me develop physically. All my teeth had fallen out from poor hygiene and the drugs. My mouth was so bad, I used to just reach in and pull out a tooth. I got my dentures and you could not tell me anything. I started buying clothes again. I always was a good dresser before the lights went out totally in my life. I was looking good and you know you are different when people acknowledge you. Women started to speak. My penis started to truly come alive. I was starting to find redemption and peace within.

I had a sponsor that I reported what was going on with me daily. He asked me to write why I think I started using and I wrote a book. When I showed him what I had written, he threw it in the trash can! I caught a serious case of resentment. He looked me square in the eye and said, *"You used because you wanted to."* Hello! The lights were on full blast with that comment. I got my first phone put in and was up all the time, talking and fellowshipping with everyone. I still had the nightmare with the woman living next door. At night I could hear her staging like he was sexually blowing her out the window. This was all done to irritate me. When you are seeking an alignment in your life, adversity places itself on your shoulders and whispers. It wants you to react so you can start using again or do something foolish. I had a network who helped me get through many things. I could call anyone and get support and advice on how to approach the many issues in my life.

I did meet someone who had about five years clean to my five months. We started talking and it was spiritual at first, but we both knew we wanted each other sexually. This was the first time in a while that I had a normal relationship; totally clean again since the post office young lady I mentioned earlier. D. and I began to want more from one another and I know her sponsor told her to leave me alone because as a newcomer I will go through many revelations and what might be exciting for right now, will bloom into new adventure's and desires. My own sponsor said, *"You don't need no relationship. Get a relationship with you first."* Neither of us listened to this. I recall her telling me she had not had sex with someone in years. She was always afraid of catching something. You see, when you play in those arenas in darkness anything is possible. I remember going to her house and I was in total fear. She made a point of telling me if I was not all what appeared to be I would not get in her bed again. That stayed in my head and I began having a conversation with my penis of his responsibility to bring me through this okay. *'Don't fail me!'* I was clean and sober and I can honestly say it was like I could not stop. The drugs had me so messed up I would have premature ejaculation or it just would not get hard. Yet on this occasion I loved her and she loved me something beyond comprehension and we were like two teenagers. This was special I thought, and I immediately was in love. She was smart and she helped me deal with the difficulties I was having at my home. We were a couple and she taught me so much.

I was at work when word came that my father had died. I was still new to recovery and it is times like this when people relapse. They needed me to come to Philadelphia. The woman he was with had tried to bury him but when they found out he had a son she could not do anything. I called my ex-wife Bette and we made the trip. I had saw my father in his last moments a few months earlier. I went down to share with him and to make an amends for any harm I may have caused. I told him that I loved him in my own way.

My father died alone without the care I presumed his lady was providing. My father was left dead in his apartment for two weeks and he exploded because of the heat. It was awful I thought. The same woman who was supposed to care for him was mistreating him when I last saw him alive. You see my father was a handsome guy who had a few women. I guess this was her way of controlling him because there was no one else to care for him. During the time we spent arranging to get him buried, I asked about his personal belongings only to have her say Earl left everything to her. I did not care about anything except the pictures he had of me and my daughter. There was nothing! Only his car, and she made sure I did not get my hands on that. When they rolled him in on the gurney and unzipped the black bag, it was horror. The physical body starts to turn on itself and the explosion that happened to him was evident. This could not be my father, there was lime or something on him. This was a tragic way for any person to exit their physical being. We decided to cremate and I shoved my father in the oven; there were five of us there. I delivered a eulogy of sort and that was it. Even though he was not there for me early on, I gave him his last rites as his son. I declare 'I love you' I said, and I wrote:

Dear Father,

Even though you were not around, even though I needed you, even though I cursed you many times, even though when darkness had me in its grip, even though I blamed you for all my misfortunes, I forgive myself, and you. I love you even though. Rest in peace.

Lady D. and I started having some great times. Things were prospering as my attitude was in the process of continued change. My thinking was better and she was a boost for me. I thought her and I were going to be married. Then the main thing which keeps people divided showed up. Our separation was all because of me and religious innuendoes. In the rooms of Narcotics

Anonymous at that time, a lot of people practiced the religion of Islam. I had first joined the Nation of Islam long ago, a different ideology for sure. I ran around with the bowtie and bean pies as fast as I could, after I was somewhere getting high or doing illegal stuff. It was all front. You should never be a part of something without taking time to think on why you are doing it.

Lady D. and I would eventually go our way because I allowed people to influence me saying I needed a Muslim wife. I gave her an ultimatum; either she becomes a Muslim or goodbye. Well, she decided she was not and I was free. Everything she had done for me, and I just kicked her as hard as I could. Some of us do that I presume. After we are helped upward, we forget those who helped carry our load. This illustrated that I still faced many issues life was presenting me with. Just because one is not taking drugs, the adjustments to the thinking is foremost the most important part of growing and developing. Here was someone who cried with me, introduced me sexually to what it meant to be made love to, helped me in every part of my newfound living, and I just acted out in a way unbefitting and unkind. I think back on all this and I had heard she talked about me for a while in the rooms of the pain I had caused her. People got tired of hearing it. I also heard she had entered into an alternative lifestyle. I knew when we were together that this was always a troubling for her. She would only go so far whenever mentioning that part of her. Some ignorant people suggested my dismissal of the relationship caused her to seek other women. I do not buy that. It may have given opportunity to act on the inclinations that were present long before I came along. It is like many things in life; we either blame or justify our decisions through external situations that take part in our lives. Like myself, I always had a host of people, places, and things I laid blame on, but in the end I did what I did because I chose to.

I used to hear about her from time-to-time. I knew one day I would have to face her and begin a dialogue to seek to make an amends of sort. The moment came as her partner, who I used to see at times at my job taking care of business said to me, *"D. wants you to contact her."* I was shocked! She knew I had a relationship with D at one time but we both never went there to even bring her up. I had no idea why she wanted to speak to me, but I called her anyway. It was about business. She thought I had completed my PhD – which I had not. I told her I would like to help her anyway and she came to my office. For the short time she was there, I was able to explain my actions and tell her how wrong I was at that time in my life. We both became a little teary eyed and it ended well. I can say, God sends you people at times when you least expect it.

There are moments when you are going through something or your heart may be broken and something to tell you it will be alright comes down your road. I want to honor and thank Lady D. for breathing into me the courage to face all the distractions that surfaced. And of course, I want to thank her for reassuring me that I was adequate sexually and it was always in my head. Most of the time, situations are not as they appear it is only our thoughts which create the drama and other entanglements we face. Bless her. I wish her well.

Confessions on Paper

I sold parts of me that I could survive the game of life. My soul was corrupted with evil flourishing throughout. I was a soldier in the army of degradation while hating life and myself in so many situations. I did things I'm not very proud of; yet they are behind this creature of habit. I lurked in the darkness like some hideous monster. Standing in corners with my mind racing about. It never bothered me how dirty I was or if I died – I was a bunch of lies. I only wanted to confess my sins, feelings of shame. You see, I have been carrying in my luggage for such a long time. I unpack these insanities from time-to-time to relieve my suffering – this happens so hear my confessions so I can get better.

CHAPTER 5
WHAT ABOUT GOD?

Religion

I was never made to go to church and my mother seldom went. She was a member at Ebenezer Baptist Church in Orange, New Jersey. I used to go on Easter and that was it. I always had a difficult time understanding God back then. I mean, why would He allow me to be going through what I went through and not take His mighty hand and get rid of the sinners who damaged my life? How could He permit the suffering of slavery, the Holocaust and the list goes on and on.

So this disposition of mine was pretty nasty towards God early on. Even after I went to the mountain I still questioned why He took so long, until I thought about all the moments He protected me. The gun put to my head, the robberies and assaults that have happened as a result of being in the wrong place at the wrong time – He had to be with me. I know that now but I still was confused as hell about religion over all.

The first religious sect I joined was the Nation of Islam. I enjoyed seeing those guys in their suits, bowties and shining shoes. I actually bought the hype that the white man was the devil after being indoctrinated. I needed someone to blame for my misgivings. I sold the paper, and as mentioned earlier, got high whenever I could. I was a fraud. I loved the discipline and structure. The social aspects of the religion are noteworthy, but the overall ideology is shot.

It is a racquet where there is some good in pointing out the wrongs and social ills; but overall there are those that eat well and those who are the dream catchers. They are the followers who keep slaving so the hierarchy can eat, sleep and live good. I stayed for a short period before I became clean.

The most amazing gift I received was the spiritual principles of Narcotics Anonymous. Religion was nowhere to be found and it was a launching point for where I am today. I enjoyed those principles. There was controversy over a Muslim being involved with an organization saying the Serenity Prayer and listening to people spew their wrongs and the difficulties they face staying straight. I made over 500 meetings and eventually was in charge of one of the meetings in Newark on Hawthorne Avenue which later moved to Clinton Avenue. I was enjoying this newfound life.

I started practicing Orthodox Islam. After having a few platonic relationships with exceptionally nice women, I decided because of listening to others, I wanted a Muslim wife. I just had to have a Muslim wife – like wanting a pair of new sneakers. It was like the obsession for something was still inside of me. There are times where our addictions transfer into other people, places and things.

I was a trash man and part of my pick-up was at a Muslim home in Newark. I got to know the people and they had a daughter who was recently divorced. She was 15 years younger and my ego was out of control. The issue was my background. They thought as they should have, I was a risk. Now I can see their side, but back then I caught resentment and was damn mad. I had the attitude that I was to have her one way or another – she was game. In 1991 she and I had sex at the Howard Johnson on Evergreen Place in East Orange, New Jersey. Now, I had no idea she would get pregnant. She was pregnant and I, wanting to do the right thing insisted we had to get married and not tell. I went to her family and they said, *"Sure…"* not knowing she was pregnant. *"Go take an HIV test."* I said, *'Excuse me?'* They said *"Go do that and we will consider your proposal."* I was scared because my history of shooting drugs came into play. With the shit I had been through, I condemned myself right there on the spot. I went to St. Michaels and found the courage to take the test and know that the shit is coming back positive. I am doomed! My kid she is carrying is infected and I infected her. All kinds of crazy thoughts ran through my head.

When they said to come in to get the results, I cried and thought about all the crap I had done and now this is my fate. When the nurse walked through the door and said negative, it was as though the whole world was lifted and I could not wait to tell her parents and show them the results; little did I know my troubles were just beginning. When I informed them of the results, they still said no, I could not marry her. Now I am trying to do things in a religious way but she is pregnant; they did not know and I am trying to save face. I had no idea what the community would think about this dirty ole man getting a 22-year old girl pregnant. It was a race against time and I finally just said the hell with this and we went to New York and got married on Broadway between 27th and 28th Street. It was in a wholesale building, took a couple of minutes and that was that.

My son was born on October 14, 1992 and he was a beautiful baby boy. We lived in my house in Irvington first. Eventually we moved to Washington Street in East Orange, New Jersey; where we set about making our marriage work. I bought her a car as part of her dowry and I settled into being this Muslim husband. I was truly unhappy though. I think it was our age difference. I needed a woman and I now had my son, her son from a previous marriage, and she was a kid herself basically.

I picked up a second job at New Community Nursing Home on South Orange Avenue in Newark plus sold tapes and anything else to provide. In Islam the man has to maintain his spouse. She can help, but it is not her responsibility to provide for the household. I tried at one time to recreate her into what I want her to be, but it just was not working. I decided to leave and hook back up with D and appease my appetite for sex. I just was not comfortable with my wife. This was my second marriage and I got what I prayed for. It was a nightmare that I did little investing in. One day I came by and she held my son up to the window and I knew I could not do what my father had done. I had to be there. I had to be a father to my children. The negative whisperer in my head said, *'You can still have a relationship with your son and not be with her,'* but something inside said I had to be there. My wife had issues in her life and we were two individuals, together just because we wanted something to hold onto.

I too was always questioning myself, some of the ramblings and conversation of those who were a couple of generations up from physical slavery themselves. They would disrespect those who died giving their lives for justice. This really turned me off. I used to sit and listen to people tell me who was in hell because they were not Muslims and how we do not have any connection with the multitudes of sacrifice made so they could live in some areas of Essex County. My biggest concern as I sat there and saw people who I shot drugs with in shooting galleries, were now all of a sudden taking on the identify of an Arab. I was always a problem child of sort because some things did not make any sense. How you can step over those who are your own ethnicity; I could never come to terms with. The foreign Muslims honored those of their particular lineage, but us here want to be everything and everyone but ourselves. There is nothing but greatness with all religions. Its rules and those that implement the policies of some of the things I heard, I was just not going with it. I guess this is why I struggled with religion and I was caught up in wanting to be a part of, looking outwardly for fulfillment when the divine is right here within me.

I change my name to Hassan Amin and wore the Kufi. I was known in the community by that name. I was still struggling in growing emotionally. There are vast regions of this world I was still ignorant about and my soul longed for knowledge. I never wanted to go overseas and study Islam, like some people did and hungered for. Bless them. I wanted to discover me. I had become a derelict, one who abandons himself. I wanted to know what life meant for me outside of Islam. I saw people parade around as though they were pure and their hearts are blackened – some of the craziness I observed. It is like people accepting faith but they bring themselves into the equation, thinking garments and attire will cure their behavior. I guess we all look outside for something to help us find sanctuary, but all we get is the same us. Change is difficult for sure. I know.

Privately I was struggling with being average. I was not challenging myself to be all I could be. It was as though I was living the way others wanted me to live. I had wasted 25 years of my life just about, and now I was stuck in mediocrity. I had another child, my youngest daughter Ibaadah. I loved her so much because it gave me a chance to be dad to a girl that I was not to my oldest daughter. I had the opportunity to make what we call in Islam, Umra Hajj in the offseason. I and my wife went with her family. We went to Egypt and what an experience that was for me. Here I was someone accustomed to abandoned buildings and puncturing my arms. Now I am in the ruins of the land of Moses. It was amazing and so memorable. The Sphinx and the Cairo museum fascinated me!

While working at New Community, I discovered the person who helped change my life forever. I first spied her while I was mopping the floor. She was beautiful and elegant. Her name was Shirley Ann Jones Davis. She had come there to visit her sister who worked there. Here I was, a married Muslim with a family, and I was interested in having her on my road. We began a conversation and she asked, *"Why are you walking behind a garbage truck and working in the nursing home? You know you're worth more than that."* she said. There were not many instances in my life where people thought I had something worth offering to life. What a confidence booster! I fell in love with her on the spot.

Shirley was a teacher and someone who I truly felt, cared for me. She had motherly love qualities and I was raw. I also was very much married. I was not happy being married because I was not getting what I needed; personal growth. Being married and religiously committed was not fitting too well. I believed in Islam, but not the presentation being applied by those who were supposed to know. I could not connect the dots between 1400 years ago (the plight of establishing the religion), and the tragedies and casualties that were among us today. There were other discrepancies and disagreements I had also.

While in Egypt and Saudi Arabia, Shirley was always on my mind. She thought I would get overseas and forget about her. I could not. She had something for me that was intriguing and formidable. My wife's family knew I was about to make a radical change and set about trying to keep me with their daughter. I bought an over garment (Muslim womenswear) to give to Shirley when I returned to the USA. When we did return, I decided to exercise my right as a Muslim man and take on another wife. This was an unacceptable subject. Most Muslim men do it for sexual reason. Some do it for the same reason I did; to set straight a compromised situation. All parties agreed to my marrying Shirley. We also found out my wife had gotten pregnant with my youngest son Fareed, in Saudi Arabia.

Being married to two women was challenging. You are supposed to be able to maintain both households. Shirley knew I could not take care of her, so what little bit I gave her was sufficient. Shirley was 12 years older than I was. She had a fabulous home in Old Bridge, New Jersey and was well off. I spent four nights with the kids and three with Shirley, whose name I changed to Nur. She and I went to Egypt and Saudi Arabia as a wedding present or dowry. We went through so much getting back into the Kingdom because I had just been there. The trip was special. Things were existing, but I was becoming overwhelmed in dealing with two wives, Nur (Shirley) said I would have to make a choice because she was not going to continue this uncertain relationship. The children's mother was pregnant and I decided to divorce her which made me the bad guy just like back when I was a kid. I was scorned and frowned upon because I only wanted to do what was best for me. It was a trying moment because the whole Muslim community turned its back on me. It got so bad they beat Nur up on Branford place, right outside the Masjid! This was the beginning of me understanding what Nur had always told me, *"Don't let people use you as a doormat."* I wanted to live and take care of my children, but I never wanted to be average. All my life I had been doing what others wanted me to do, and for once in my life I decided I was hungry for more.

Moving Forward

Nur and I struggled, but she continued to push me to go to school. She saw my education as a way for us to prosper and for me to raise my conscious level. She had lost her son when he was just 22-years old and she was giving me what she wanted to put into him. She was doing so well before she met me that she was negotiating to purchase a realty insurance firm for six million dollars and had the backing. She was brilliant, but first she had this pup on her hand to elevate. When I say I was raw, I was. She basically took the foundation that was there and shaped me. Walking, talking, networking, how to stand and to stop using my fingers to push my food on my fork. I had so much to learn because I still had so many street ways. I started writing about everything and she encouraged it as a therapy. Below I wrote some of the things I shared with only her; about the secrets I always kept inside.

Eye on Me

I remember a time when I wandered throughout the lands in search of meaning and purpose in my life. I had looked towards the heavens asking why I had such unhappiness and pain attached to me. I felt so indifferent and my soul was shattered; unable to grasp anything worthy. I cried my eyes out as winters coldness added to my hopelessness. A part of me wanted to just lie down and surrender; to quit life and its unfairness and troublesome woes. My mother had long asked me to just believe and to give God's salvation a chance to change my heart. I was afraid I did not believe He cared for me...nor did I think He even considered my pain. You see, I had been everything one may desire to loathe. Iniquity had stitched itself into my soul and took apart any faith I ever had.

I had once crawled out of an alleyway on my knees beaten by the elements and life's hardships. I did everything unwilling and killing me was an option I pursued strongly. I was confused and chose to languish on my knees. When I strolled along looking at the monster I had become, a part of me wanted something – what, I did not know, but something was missing.

I was an adult yet a child who seemed to have lost his way along the corridors of life. I think it began when I turned away from my Lord and found refuge in sin and wickedness. I transformed myself into a creature unbecoming and undesirable, yet the Lord still loved me, something I did not understand. The saga continued as I came within an inch of destroying myself. God sent to me a bouquet of faith. It arrived on a day when the sky serenaded my existence and an invitation of hope renewed my soul. I fell upon the ground and screamed as this cloak of evil was removed. I heard the lyrical sweetness of a voice blessing me and it baked me in a lake of mercy where I rose after being dead. My awakening, how blessed I have been. And as I rose and began to follow the light, I turned to see the abuse I had endured…the suit of pain and all the ungodly things I had done laying there no longer a part of me. Grace took my hand and I ascended and clouds of forgiveness showered me as I now knew my Lord who had always kept a watchful eye on me.

Broken Spirits

Sometimes our spirits are broken, shattered and scattered across the plains of no resolutions. I myself have been subjected to difficulty at times as it intertwined itself into my heart. During these periods of unrest, I found myself questioning life and wishing for a way to escape. In my reprieve from these moments I only found refuge in broken promises, which I have made to myself. You see, I have been a procrastinator because of fear. Fear has held me prisoner throughout my life. It is my jailer…it dictates to me. In a darkened room where fear held me enslaved, I sat in a corner quiet not wanting to add to the anguish I have always felt. My story begins when visitors came to me when I was a child, latching onto me and having their way.

It disturbed me so much; I carried the fear these escapades would bring for such a long time. Each time there was company in our home; I would brace myself in a corner in the dark. I knew someone would make their way to my room and assault me. I was afraid to tell and would only remain still as I was grappled about and made to perform on a stage of lewdness.

My captivity is self-imposed these days at times, as I still find it hard to trust. Many days I still listen for footsteps in the dark. I clench my sheets sometimes when something unexpected walks into the dark with me. It could have been a loved one, but those buried feelings of fear unravel me. The only thing, which has rescued me, is faith…with its security; faith has beamed a light of hope for this lost soul of many parables. I know one thing for sure I have been tarnished, and until I fully accept it as an unfortunate incidence in my life I will always be afraid, especially of the dark with its jailer; fear.

Nur strongly encouraged my writing because she knew I was still dealing with emotional disturbances inside; splinters from days of old. Sometimes we think leaving drugs alone will solve the problems. I still did not know why I cried at times for no good reason. I was just learning to be civil and appreciative. She gave me so much courage and instilled in me the reason to live. I went to school and it was a whole new world. The more I went to school, the more my eyes started to open. Listening to religion as a way of life was not my future. I wanted so much of what life had for me to discover. I wanted to smell the world with my eyes closed and never again separate myself from anyone based on text or policies. She embraced my children and I have no doubt I would have had many more children had I not made that decision to leave. It was difficult because it tore my children in half for over 22 years.

My kids were in the middle of a tug-of-war between their mothers and her parents and me. It was such a war of ignorance and selfishness that it took its toll and I, like the many of people of African descent too, consistently dealing with family court, restraining orders, resentments and anger. It was so stressful that Nur said we had to leave New Jersey. I did not want to go because I had made supervisor for the City of Newark. I was seeing to the needs of the Islamic community and I was building a name for myself. Even with all this to process, I was still consistently working on me. I was haunted in some respect for what I went through. Acceptance and forgiveness is such a key to moving forward – it is not easy! In order to remedy your life, you have to find for yourself what heals you. This is why I always felt the need to search beyond what appeared to me. This hunger inside was burning. I still looked at the time I had wasted and could never recover. There's a saying; *"You can get more money, but you can't get more time."*

This move Nur wanted to do in relocating south, I just did not want to do. She took one look at then Governor Bush, with his announcement to run for president and made it clear we would lose everything we have, or she had, if he became president. Her money was invested in a diversity portfolio and that being the case, she would have lost a tremendous amount of her savings. I was still reluctant to leave because I was climbing immensely on my job, with her pushing me to say I want to be a supervisor. I just did not see me leaving. I questioned her one day and she said to me something that still stays in my thoughts. She said, *"They will never allow you to go no further than where you are now."* I said, 'You're crazy! Do you see my picture in City Hall? Plus I am in charge of the whole downtown area. You have to be nuts.' I asked her why she thought they would not let me go any further. She said, *"Because of who you are and your disposition."* I was shocked she would say this!

She went on to explain that these quests of becoming greatness, with integrity and principles, some people are uncomfortable with those having decency and respect for others. I had no problem of stepping on people at one time, but now I was afraid to do any harm because of what I represented and what I was becoming. I am not an angel then or now, but I do not sell me anymore. This same persona I possess today is genuine and it is a virtue of my mothers' who I always thought was weak. This kindness I have is something I hated back then. I was people pleasing and just wanted friends; someone to like me. I was seeking approval and that in itself has been a muscle I have always had to work on. I just want to be decent and my views today are one of ownership for one's life. I was never before responsible for me, and I guess this is why I feel people have greatness. It is only our ignoring ourselves which causes us to juggle through life pointing the finger.

We were arranging to leave New Jersey, and at that time I had custody of my oldest son and daughter. My baby son was with his mother because he was being breastfed. Let me explain how I got custody: When a Muslim woman marries again; the former husband has the right to request his kids, especially if it is a girl. This was another tug of war situation. When we left for Georgia with all our belongings I still was employed by the City of Newark and had to come back to finish my Associates Degree until that March. There was a court hearing and once again I went before a judge but this time I was accused of removing my kids out the State of New Jersey without the State being aware. This became a nightmare and I had to get a lawyer. I had to petition the courts and it worked out. The sadness in all this is how my children's mother could not see the better life someone else was offering. All she could see and hear from those people who always whisper in your ear, *"They taking your kids."* This is what estranged our relationship for over two decades. Selfishness, hatred because I left, the list goes on; is what kept me from moving past what should have been let go of.

I got all my kids and now we were in Georgia and I still was a work in progress. Nur, my wife, was in reality raising my kids and me. I was still awfully raw. I got lost in Georgia in some respect but it gave me and my kids a chance to see differences and experience a new way of living. People who were always in our bed, as they say, were not around. We settled in and it was beautiful. We were the only Blacks living in our community and that did not go well when we first moved in, but I had the best lawn on our property. I took care of it extremely well and it showed.

Nur, being 12 years older than me, was insecure sometimes. I was blooming but had not reached that distinguished manly look. People thought I was her son. This made her mad and upset. She treated me like a son, too. It became a burden at times dealing with her regiments. There were other females and I always gave it a thought to act out, but Nur was good to me. This ascension would not be had she not placed me in the right frame of mind and showed me how to present myself. There was someone I had seen back in New Jersey who was much younger and I always wanted her to *'breathe on me.'* We both worked for the City of Newark. I thought I was out of my league. I was a practicing Muslim and she just looked seductive and tempting. We became friends and even when I moved back to New Jersey, I teased her from time-to-time, to *'breathe on me.'* I would later get together with this woman after returning to New Jersey; well after Nur and I parted. I never knew that in all the years I had known this younger woman that I would care and fall in love with her as I did. She meant something to me, but sometimes what we may want may not be for us. I will just say SH is someone who I will always pray and hope the best for.

Things became extremely tough in Georgia with having a house built from the ground up, kids, school, and trying to work. My wife and I started to argue and my kids were in the middle. I slept most of time in the den and was lonely. I think there comes a time in marriages or relationships or even at a job where you cannot grow anymore. Everything becomes routine and stagnation breathes on you and you want out. I wanted to go and I knew this and she knew this.

I completed my MBA with a specialization in Healthcare Management. I graduated at the Georgia World Congress Center in downtown Atlanta. The guest speaker was an electrifying woman who inspired me to challenge life. You know when it is time to go because the student starts to challenge the teacher. My wife was a great business woman and pushy. I pushed back and she would start to be somewhat mean to me and my kids. Not hurting them physically, but not doing my daughters hair which left me going nuts trying to comb it.

I worked briefly for the Georgia Department of Labor. After being laid-off we started using our charge cards. My credit was seven and some change, but it was a real challenge to pay the bills. Nur always had an answer, and I started my PhD program in 2004. I stayed in school getting more in debt with student loans to get money to pay the bills. When the economy is bad you go to school. I went online to Walden University and finished with a respectable 3.9 GPA. I was almost ready, but there were still feelings of emptiness inside. I loved my kids and I loved Nur, but when alone, I still wanted to know all there was for me to know. I was unfulfilled and vacant in a certain part of my life. The journey had gotten much better, but I still struggled with what it all meant.

I did not practice Islam any longer even though we prayed together. I just did not get it. Even before we left New Jersey, for my efforts around the masjid on Branford Place, I was afforded a first class ticket to make the Hajj as an invited guest of the King. I flew Saudi Air from Dulles Airport and in going through the rituals, being grateful, and almost being filled, I still privately asked, *'What does it all mean?'* Once again I felt I was experiencing things outside of me to bring salvation or some relief, yet I was alone in my sentiments. I knew when I went to the masjid, with all the greatness the religion is, I could not accept the thoughts of those I was around a lot of times. The feelings that human life among those who died for righteousness did not matter, bothered me. This was the hardest thing for me to accept. I sat quietly many times wondering do people actually know who they are. I tried being not me for years; an addict, a bum, a wino, the list goes on and on. I was tired of wearing masks, of being someone I was not.

There was a guy I knew from a shooting gallery in New York, and now here he was talking as though he was Grande with rags on and a staff. I said, *'My brother, what happened?'* He went to tell me he was practicing Islam like I was. Unlike him, I was not going to start imaging an Arab – no offense to Arabs. I think African-American people emulate everything but themselves. We take on identities we think defines us and most of the time it is something which impressed you and it is easier to not find yourself and being other than, by settling for mediocrity and what is unworthy. I was on something different. Common sense, something my wife said I needed, had started to reveal itself to me. There were some things I just would no longer do. Even my children, who I love and have Muslim names, were never made by me to feel as though they had to be Muslim. My kid's mother, grandparents and cousins are Muslim, but I always wanted my kids to be whatever they wanted to be. I saw how so many young Muslim children were forced and when they got older they rebelled, like all kids do when you do not give them diversity.

Being disillusioned with Islam and not wanting to be married started bubbling up inside me. My kids used to cry whenever I had to go out and leave them. I think they were intimidated by my Nur. She treated them good but stern. Every time we would take them to New Jersey for the summer vacation they would cry all the way back to Georgia. Their mother loved them and all their family was in New Jersey, but there were no rules. The structure was not as tight as that ship in Georgia. My wife did not leave anything out of place. They had chores and obligations. Cleaning their showers and rooms were expected in Georgia. When they got to New Jersey, none of that went on. My wife was from the old school. It began to take its toll on me. I was almost ready I thought, and an opening came when we disagreed about something concerning the kids and I made an agreement which I would live to regret; to send them back to their mother. I will not ever forget the day I prepared a flight for them. On that day, I was unhappy and I immediately blamed my wife for her oppression on my kids and myself. Her friend had told her as long as the kids were there I would stay put and she was so correct. After delivering them to their mother, I planned to find a way out.

Nur took me on a cruise, another new experience she introduced to me. It was fabulous! We took more trips, driving from Georgia to Florida, and also to New Orleans. With Nur, there were many moments of growth for me. She taught me things that I needed to be aware of. I recall being at an event and a guy who remembered me from the street was trying to remember himself to me. Nur got wind of it and asked to speak to me. When we were alone she said, *"Stupid! If people are not sure they know you, don't remind them."* It was always a lesson to reinforce me. Things were beginning to crumble.

I met a Muslim woman with whom I had a brief affair. The bills were piling up and I was about to start my dissertation for my PhD in Public Heath, with focus on Community Health. Along with these stressors, Nur was getting older and starting to ail. I looked for jobs in Georgia, but not only was there a good ole white boys network, but an African-American one, too. You cannot get in on either unless you are from there. The south takes its time in just about everything. I was amazed how I never heard a horn blow where we lived at. Traffic was a nightmare and decisions are made when they feel like it. It was a comfortable environment if I had cash flow. My children being back in their mom's hands worried me. I was concerned all the time. I would call and it was upsetting; plus my thoughts of her being as unstable as my own stuff was. I just wanted out. I decided to look for work in New Jersey.

My first wife's brother died and I travelled north to New Jersey for the funeral. It was good seeing my kids but the glow and healthiness they once had was now replaced with uncleanliness. As my wife in Georgia would say right away, *"They are not clean."* It is comical but I used to think people were clean because they were of the same faith or because they looked kempt. Nur reminded me that they were not clean. She was like that. She would take me out and show me wealthy and those that have a little money. She had an inclination and intuition for sure.

I embraced my kids and did not want to go back to Georgia. The school they were in was a nightmare. They lived in gang neighborhoods and I was bothered like hell. As soon as I would get back to Georgia, I would be out; one way or another. I would do all I can to continue to support my wife, but I wanted out. A job opened up at the local college and I made plans. I had been in contact with someone who was running the campaign for Mayor of Newark. I must say that one of the most remarkable politicians I had met was the Honorable

Sharpe James. I worked for him and it is because of him giving me a leave of absence to attend school in Georgia I am always indebted. I admire him for having the courage to do the things he did. The next man is the now Senator Cory A. Booker, who as mayor added value to my life too. The charisma these two people possess is outstanding. I was told to come back to get involved. I came back and interviewed, but I did not get the job and was told to stay and wait. Although Senator Booker was elected I had to wait to get hired.

Damaged Goods

The illicit affair with the bringer of unkind advances sent my world upon the spiral down case towards the lower elements on the corners of no return. I was so young with the whole world in front of me. I chose to play the game from the insanity point of view, walking the streets in circumferences bounded by no restraints. This began with the harboring of my desire to not deal with reality, instead looking for shortcuts and ways to cover my guilt and shame, which presided over me. The time it took to disguise the real me, eventually stitched me up so no one could see me. The pain and agony in working towards my demise left me in the caverns of hopeless dreams. The pressure I carried as well as my family's tears drenched me into the pit of smokeless fire within the soul of this fool.

My destiny changed upon the trauma, which inflicted me, leaving me grasping for my breath day-to-day. I would submerge myself between the paraphernalia in my pockets to sitting against walls of harden hearts looking to understand me. It had gotten to the point where I could not remember the real me. The real me was displaced in some trunk underneath the good which I truly am. The hours would pass along with days and nights, still my growth and development were fastened by my inability and choice of not to grow as well as feel. The shock, which rocked me back to unraveling this, damaged goods are a testament of the power, which is beyond my control.

Here I was an arm's length away from the fire when suddenly I pivoted and began my journey towards the throne of prosperity. The search for me has had its wonders and limitations. I know I am within me; somewhere the person whose maturity was stunted by my traumatic experiences. I have learned to love others and me. I want to know me!

Realizing in the aftermath of my destructible way in which I survived, I am not a damaged apparel of any sort. The goodness which expands my nature is finally in place once again submitting to life on each and every day. If you want to know about the shame and guilt brought about by the evil, which molested me, I have accepted the enviable of that situation and forgiven me first and those who I may have harmed.

I hope you will pray for me and smile when you finish reading this knowing I have made it back from the isles of damaged goods to be who I most certainly am which is a servant of humility giving myself a chance to live.

CHAPTER 6
JUST AROUND THE BEND

Homeless Again

From March 2006 until February 2007 I spent 90 percent of my time in my truck. I stayed a couple of weeks with my oldest daughter which ended in a disaster. I stayed with my wife's cousin for a while until it was time to go. I slept at Dunkin Donuts in East Orange, New Jersey and at 4th Avenue in the same town. I would shower in the masjid; they let me stay there for a while until I was no longer welcomed because of the antics of a Muslim brother who wanted his fighter to stay in there too. So I had to go, and in the street I went. I ate when I could and got gas money from here and there. It was trying. I was losing weight and concerned about my wife in Georgia. I knew I would never return though. I needed to be near my children to protect them, and to make sure their lives were safe. It was such a bad time. A Christian woman of such wonders gave me a blanket and a few dollars to survive. It seemed as though we always have to be shown everyone you think will be there for you will not. I was writing my dissertation: *Looking at HIV between Muslim and Christian Women*. The IRB did not think I would be able to do this because a qualitative methodology was not going to happen, because that kind of conversation was not going to happen.

The more I went through on this journey, the more growing I was able to do. I think we are broken at times to be rebuilt – to toughen us for the next chapter in our lives. I was lying across the front seat of my truck unhappy again asking God why. Why had He brought me so far to be homeless? I could have given up and went to Georgia to a very nice home, but that was not an answer. I needed to reinvent me. I needed to find a way to draw attention to myself. I was a guy with a story, now educated, and away from the gutter thinking way of life.

I also met R. – a woman I was so crazy about that I would stand on a corner every morning just to see her sparkle and wave to me. We began a conversation and in fairness, as the relationship increased I sought a divorce from my wife in Georgia. I pronounced divorce and said I will always be there to do what I could, but I wanted no attachments. I recall when R. brought me some soup and she met me at Dunkin Donuts. She was shocked I was homeless. I was the cleanest homeless guy you ever want to see. I also began to up my writings to cover social issues and romance. I just loved writing to women and was pretty good. Some women I wrote to online thought I was another woman because men just do not take their time and be as gentle as I am.

I was finally able to get an Adjunct teaching position at the local community college. The money was minimal but I did my best. I moved in with a Muslim brother and the job came through from the City. I started in the Health Department. I also got notices about child support because the relationship between my children's Mom and me was estranged and becoming worse. I had no real reason to dislike her, but the harm she was trying to do to me became ugly. It was always back and forth, the kids in between suffering. I went to Family Court so much for child support, and I always gave. My taxes were taken when they should not have been. I never received a dime for all the years my kids were in my custody. Even after a violent offense happened involving my children and their mother, I got custody and still was responsible for the arrears. That is the way it goes. I was called by my daughter and went to the house with the police. My daughter had been violently beaten. I was angry and asked myself, *'When does life smooth itself?'* All I have ever known is tribulations and despair. I finally got custody of my children. Now what do I do with them?

R.

R. stepped up to help out with my kids. I always thanked her. She did something great for me and I was truly appreciative. We had a strange relationship like all my affairs. You see, I sometimes think I am this movie star, like Clark Gable or Cary Grant. I now understand I have never had a relationship with me which plays into the equation. I really treat women as they should be. I am the kind of guy who will put his jacket down so the puddle from the water will not get on their feet; chivalrous. I have tried to understand why I am always making sure the woman I am with is alright. I have a tremendous giving heart. I have been told I give my power away trying to make up for my mistreatment of my Mom. I have no idea. I have never known how it feels to truly be physically alone, my own apartment, doing my own dishes, just being with me. I was either with my Mom, married or in an institution. I know of no other way to treat people especially women except as a queen. I honor me or do I? If I did, I asked myself, *'Then why forget me, to ensure everyone else is okay?'* I struggled with this and my wife in Georgia used to say, *"Your road lost time. You did not have a normal progression through life. You never experienced going from one stage to the next. It was interrupted by insanity and pain."* I had to take a look at that because I was a young man questioning whether I was adequate to be with a woman my age. Why was I so comfortable with older, and I do mean older women. Most of those women when I was just a kid, either acted like they were sleep or was drunk. Those women were prey to me as I was preyed upon. I guess so much goes into the psyche of why we do the things we do.

My love affair with R was strange – with me being made to think it is not time, and wait, or I am involved conversations. She was hooking me in and I made sure I did all I could to be nice to her, because I wanted love.

The same things which drew me into using drugs and the other calamities in my life transfer it into me still looking for something outside of me to love me and give me relief. Bottom line; I wanted to be loved and I found myself doing everything for someone else just to get them to appease me; just be with me way of thinking. All my life I have chased after acceptance from women and people with religion. There is a list of things I have regret about, but I have forgiven me.

My life with R. became a comfort for her and distracted me from my tiredness of being unfulfilled. I was so involved emotionally with her that I would come walk her daughter's dogs (I loved the little guys), make her oatmeal, take her two blocks to her job, pick her up every day and drive back two blocks. Gentleman yes, but it can be unhealthy. People need space and it did not matter to her. I just got tolerant of the relationship; immune, and I was not growing on her either, I presume.

I ended what maybe should have never been. Another lesson in putting others in front of me so I would not have to deal with me. I came to know unhappiness again. I felt seeking out external situations to make me happy, a temporary fix – I find with me, I look towards others to inflame me. For some strange reason, it was hard for me to give myself a chance. Maybe I never thought I was good enough. Maybe I was still hearing echoes of *"You are not shit, never going to amount to nothing, your mother should have gotten rid of you."* – I have no idea. I tried to convince myself but deep down inside I was unfulfilled because of me. I always poured just enough expecting others do to the rest. That is where my anguish and sufferings are. In a vase I refused to fill.

A Cleansing

My day started off like most days with me feeling despondent and lost on some plateau of never ending circumstances. I have no idea at times why this scenario of hopeless questions and complications latches onto my soul. I have tried to forgive everything which may be a cause to my harrowing situation yet resolutions are evasive and I continue to search for absolutions of some sort. My unhappiness starts with me, for I make the choices about choosing between happiness and sadness. I choose to sit in-between both worlds and flow with whatever is suitable for the time; this is disturbing because uncertainty is an acquaintance of kind who keeps me in a dungeon of indecisiveness. What awaits me is a mystery in itself for the trends of my forecast is lost in a chest hidden away from my heart. I await the finality to my presence in this world and hope tomorrow will be forthcoming, and I will decide to ride on a feather of courage. My strength will come when I can shut the door of my past, lock it, walk away, and accept His Grace; otherwise I will be buried along with the rest who never found the Lord.

Utilizing Me

I was part of a reentry program for the City of Newark which I feel honored to be an originator. It is something when life presents pictures of reality to you. Some of the roads I had been on has always been the unexpected to be sent your way. I was a single parent and struggling and I was presented with a lay-off notice, and as fast as I was presented the notice, I was presented an invitation to stay through a new money stream. This took place not because of someone of my own ethnicity or religious faith – this happened because of someone white. You see what I found out along the corridor of life, color does not matter to me. In reality it is the content of your character and what you present. Everyone has divines in them but conceal it with evil and other damnations. It is always someone who you hardly know that is sent to help you and to provide you with what God wants you to do. I was very fortunate to grow to a level of accepting people for who they were. In my job we all were charged with helping those coming home from prison. It was an interesting appointment because I believe those of us charged had issues ourselves to solve or to discover. The then Mayor Cory A. Booker did an amazing thing in formulating an official reentry platform for those coming home from incarceration. I would be remiss if I did not mention that former Mayor of Newark, the Honorable Sharpe James, had an unofficial prison reentry program as well. He hired a lot of people coming out of the penal system. I thank God for both these men as well as the councilpersons who worked alongside them.

The one thing I wanted to do when writing about my journey is acknowledging those who I always looked to as an example and not attack anyone. Attacking only separates people. I have nothing bad or questionable to say about anyone. I even cleared the air with my former in-laws and my ex-wife. I declared completion with my father, mother and those relationships I could complete. You see, holding on to matters only keeps one stuck. I recall going to my mom's grave and screaming, falling to my knees in the dirt. I was so sorry what I had done to her. My aunt is buried underneath her as well. Yes, the journey was becoming special in some respect because my eyes were beginning to open more and I looked at life through the lens of an aging man who still had a few splinters in him, but was aging gracefully.

Helping people and going into the prison speaking of my life was becoming a passion and of course my writing. I was seeing myself in the people who came into see me. I saw in them the broken pieces. I too, shared with them. The shame and guilt and the bad decisions because of pain they made as I did. Behind closed doors many would get honest with me about many subjects I could identify with. Feeling impotent and empty, a commonality I shared. We go through life wounded and at times we are stitched together and because of feeling hopeless, we take out the thread. We do not trust the process, lose faith and find ourselves bleeding emotional pain. So many died that I knew who never had a chance to live; destroying themselves as I had tried over and over again. So many people have come into my life, for just a small part in my story and they would be gone. Some brought more pain and some tried to love me, but because I was so incapable of receiving any love, I banished them.

This job helped me to continue to heal and grow. The people around me minimally helped me to understand more and more about me. A late bloomer I am in so many ways. In losing time, I gained in different aspects of my life. I was cracked like a vase put back together. I know what it feels like to be broken. I believe this appointment was for me and for others to see that miracles do happen. I met so many interesting people; those we were seeking funds and those who just needed hope. I have a way with people because I unclothe me. I let people see that it is okay to drop their masks and to allow their heart to be open. You see, it is being fearless, courageous, and heroic to show your own flaws and moments of embarrassments. I went to work each and every day inspired to help someone to come into the light. There were times I needed a lesson on growing muscles inside and in certain areas. Self-esteem issues were still there – splinters in me.

In 2010, one of the things I did which caused a raucous was calling the Orange Police Department and saying I wanted to present the department with a plaque to honor them for locking me up over 24 years ago. The lady on the phone thought I was on drugs and transferred me to the police who too thought there is a wacko on the phone wanting to thank us for locking him up. I was serious and I even called a newspaper friend of mine to help with the story. The administration was going through some difficult times and my story helped to change the narrative in some respect. The police gave me a hard time and it was the Honorable Councilman at that time, Rayfield Morton, a childhood friend who knew my saga, arranged for me to come there.
http://blog.nj.com/njv_barry_carter/2010/03/city_hall_worker_honors_police.html

It was a memorable night when I told my story and presented the plaque. There were comments; I needed to do that for me. It made the headlines front page and people all over City Hall who did not know my story congratulated me. The judges and other police of Newark thought what an admirable thing to do. Then of course you have those haters who because it is not about them dislike or find fault. I was walking and a Muslim brother stopped me and asked. *"How come you thank the cops and not Allah (God)?"* I asked him, *'What makes you think I did not and whose soul is this anyway?'* I made the decision that I would not bite into the religion. It seemed to me that every time religion was inserted, there was nothing but policies and rules. When my children's mother and I were going through things and went to the authorities in the Masjid, it was always no resolve. They tell you do not go to the system and settle everything in the masjid, which I guess is good; but if you want justice go to the courts.

You pay taxes and that too was my argument; how people were so much against American policies, but they lived here. I always felt if you think it is better living in an Islamic country, leave. I felt as though there was no way I was going to pay taxes, and have them making decisions on my livelihood in council meetings and I not having a say so. So many foreign Muslims come to America and send their kids to the best schools and one wants to sell oil on the corner. Now do not get me wrong, but the more you study and invest in you – you grow and develop. So I guess this is why the search for me was ongoing because I would always think and do what is unpopular when I came into the light. Another moment that became progressive thinking was I started to get these epiphanies in my life since coming into the light. When I was in darkness I could not see any blessings because I was choosing to ignore God.

The Harvard Club in New York visitation was memorable, a moment where I had to challenge myself once again, to be more than. No matter how much distance was put between me and the past, different events happened where I challenged myself. You see, we have these learning lessons to prepare us and to do any restoration that may be needed. Well I experienced a moment where I had to make a decision to either retreat or go forward. I had built an amiable relationship with the Social Policy Director from the Manhattan Institute, a conservative think-tank in New York. He, my former director and I had eaten and discussed ills and social determinants plaguing inner cities. I also have established a pleasant relationship with a law professor from the University of Pennsylvania. I wanted to formerly meet this interesting law professor who signed a copy of her book and sent it to me; she was a neurosurgeon as well. So they decided to invite me to the Harvard Club; a club where you can only be a member if you attended Harvard. A date was set and I was excited. Here I was, Earl Scott, who was greasy as a Louisiana fish fry at one time, had been invited for lunch with people who genuinely wanted to entertain me.

I took the bus and got off at Port Authority in New York, an area I hustled around and used to go through to get uptown to add some insanity to my already irrational, disturbed, and psychologically misfit mind. It brought back memories. As I walked towards the Harvard Club, I passed through Times Square, and recalled sitting in the movies back then in a comatose state of mind. I got there and stood across the street from the Harvard Club, where great people who helped shape the country dined. I watched the attire and how elegant and ripened the climate was. The doorman himself looking refined and greeting people with such distinguishes. Now at this very moment the roommate we all have in our heads, the EGO started talking. It said *'what in the hell are you doing here? Are you crazy? You might as well go right on back to Port Authority and get on the bus and take your butt back home, you do not belong here.'* I pondered and my whole life flashed before me; the monster I once was, the crimes I have committed, the destruction of my marriage and ripping my mother's heart apart. I was frozen and yes, all those thoughts were hounding me. You see it is fear which freezes us from moving forward with our ideas, leaving a relationship, or just telling someone you did not appreciate the way they treated you. Fear keeps us hostage and fear did its best to get me to fold myself and hide. My past tried to get me to run.

I had been waiting to see if my host was in view obviously so they could help me go in; make it easier for me. That is the way most of us deal with situations, we want others to do it for us to cushion the pain of whatever we are going through. I had to face what I had been avoiding most of my early life; standing up for me. I walked right on over and the doorman looked at me like *"I was wondering what you were going to do."* I walked right on in through the majestic door and it was an experience I will never forget because of the lesson I needed to learn. I dined at the Harvard Club and ate in a room where the great President Theodore Roosevelt (a Harvard grad) had donated all the animal heads adorning the walls! I handled myself with honor and class. They were amazed that someone like me, who was lost and now found, is the true amazing grace. I was spared.

Corners

Corners – these places where sometimes I took sanctuary for my woes. I used to hide from my predators within the corners of my home. Head tucked down and eyes closed to not be seen, praying to myself that I would not be discovered. The corners where I laid until I believed it was safe were my world all wrapped up in so little space. The years came and my legs became longer so I moved myself from the corners to another scene. Drinking and laughing indulging to mask my fears on the corners those confines of waste, I drifted away. I lay on the pavement – people stepping over me; I was dying, my soul so confused to say the least. Time passes and the corners were still my angels of destruction. I looked with my eyes toward cloudy days where my bottle of life seemed to remedy no more. On that day as I sat on the stoop of my corner of despair I looked upward and saw the light. It was bright and a hand reached out for me. It embraced me into its bosom and washed me of my crust of fear. It told me to remove myself from this dwelling of which there is no end. Take yourself towards the mountains of hope and climb and shed your sorrows and do not look back. I started my search with anticipation of curiosity. I left the corners behind me no longer afraid of my shame and guilt. I pass the corners today with remembrance to what it was like for me. I see others in my place waiting to be free. Some will see and some will not. The light, that light, which saved me from my jail, is there for those who will be saved. So I await the last corner, which is my grave!

Then other moments came for me to add value to my life or to others. I also began writing profusely. Some I shared, others I kept to myself. I loved writing about the social ills and determinants in our societies and I was becoming a thinker; looking at things in-depth. One thing I found out was, even though I changed my life and detached from those things I no longer need attached, I was awakening.

I cracked my knee in 2010 and was suffering from arthritis as well. I had no more cartilage and one bone was rubbing against the other. I needed a knee replacement. I went into the VA Hospital in East Orange and it devastated me. Not only do I suffer from the partial knee replacement, but I stayed in the hospital for a month. Abraham Lincoln once stated if you want to test a man's character give him power. Well, if you ever want to see who your friends are get sick or have a hardship upon your shoulders. Even the woman R was not there for me. She went out of town. I never told her how upsetting it was for her to leave me.

My affairs were somewhat in order but my kids were not old enough to manage them if I was to die. That was one of many instances in my life I have come to understand that I placed myself at times in the hands of people who really did not have my best interest at heart. I was so sick; almost dying from infections and the pain was so great. I had to have four surgeries in 27 months. R was there minimally and I guess she did the best she could do. You see some people do not know how to deal with illness. I do not hold any resentment, but at that time her scorecard concerning me was receiving red ink and check marks. I went back to work too soon and on a walker. I had lost so much weight that people were reluctant to shake my hand. They looked at me like, *"You got the package."* (That is slang for HIV.) Some went immediately to wash their hands. I saw the fear in their eyes, and it was then I knew for sure, what people go through which are ill.

In preparing for surgery I had all these tests. The doctor wanted to know why my knee went bad so fast. Maybe cancer or some other disease (HIV) was his surmise. Once again my heart hit the floor and my mind roamed to all the places I had been and the at-risk behaviors I engaged in. I became fearful. We are responsible for our actions and we create lives for ourselves and at times what we invested, whether negative or positive, it shows up. Like working-out in a gym, eventually, if you are consistent, the results come through positive comments. People will say you look great or different. Then again when investing in that lifestyle out there it too has results and those arenas we play in bring back harm and other circumstances beyond our control in the end. I had done many things in my life and now I was once again facing the investments I made from two decades or more ago of trying to destroy myself.

The results came back and once more I was not HIV positive. I just inherited arthritis from the pounding I did on my leg, working on the trash truck, the falling as a kid on my knees, and playing on concrete playgrounds. All this took its toll. The day I had the surgery I had no one with me. I was dropped-off by one of my students from my adjunct work. R. had left town and I kissed my kids goodbye and that was that. I talked to God and it is a scary thing when you are having surgery. I had to do this alone and called a friend. I was wondering about taking the pain medication because they were about to cut my bone. I said I would take aspirin but it was suggested whatever they offered to take it. I had a difficult time and lost a lot of weight. I stayed a month in the hospital because of major infections almost shutting down my kidneys. I was sick and I was in pain. The damage and trauma I endured was overwhelming. I laid there in pain alone and I said I never wanted to walk again. With my partial knee replacement or any replacement they get you walking the next day. I had it difficult. In the VA Hospital they have so many people working on you. It is a teaching hospital.

The drugs had me spinning and my body got addicted when I came home. I went back to work too soon struggling down the street with a walker and in so much pain. I was catching cramps in my knee because my electrolytes where all screwed up. I too noticed how people were treating me differently because of the weight loss. They thought I had the virus and avoided me. I now understood even more how awful it feels to be treated different. No matter what your circumstance is, treating people unfair is wrong. This was yet another problem I had with the African-American community; it seems we are determined to make every issue a race issue. I wanted to say, and did, that most of the persons who helped me during crisis were not of my ethnicity. I did have a few African-Americans but the majority were people who did not look like me. This is why you get to a certain maturity and you just treat people accordingly. The race thing became and still does bother me. When I was sick the woman I thought I loved was nowhere to be found. I can think about who has always stepped-up to support my life. In going back to work too soon and eventually having to have three more surgeries took its toll. I should count my blessings, because it could have been much worse.

Death of My Wife Nur

During all these surgeries and after, Nur my former wife in Georgia, was becoming sicker. She had stage four cancer. I was a single parent and I was sending money for her to pay for the car insurance, phone and other small concerns, but I could not help keep the home intact. They foreclosed and she told me she was staying in Walmart and I collapsed. I was blown away because here is a woman who gave me a chance and helped my children, and I was powerless to this situation. My conscious brought back guilt and I just carried these feelings around hearing her cry and I was becoming depressed. I worried and even my kids were upset.

After a while she got into the senior citizen place and I would call all the time. I felt as though I had abandoned her. I walked around thinking about all I am is because of her. I was told by people, I should not carry these feelings that she knew what she was getting into. I still remained disturbed. I made the last trip down to Georgia in January 2013 and I took the kids. They had not been back in a while and I thought she would be in some shack, but she was in a nice place. I had been sending her movies, and when I saw her, her hair was gone. She did not look sick, but she was. I took her food shopping, but I wanted to get away from there as soon as possible as I may have mentioned. I wanted to change this whole story within me, should I have stayed, then what would have become of my kids. Maybe I should have persevered through it all. I left there in tears knowing I would never see her alive again. I was still communicating with her when she took a turn for the worse.

Her sister called and said she had to put her in a nursing home, and it was up to her to get well enough to come home. I said *'Okay, is there anything I should do?'* and she said *"No."* I wanted to come but she said it would not be wise. Her son and his father were there and to cut down on any kind of commotion to stay away. I felt insulted but respected the wishes. I then asked her sister what are the plans in case something happened to her. She said she had no money to bury her, but would cremate. I broke down, because Nur was Muslim to the end and this was unacceptable, but what could I do. She then told me she was not leaving the Hospice, and a day or two the most of what life had for her. I was distraught and lost it. I felt so bad and tearfully I told my kids, and the call came she passed on August 7, 2013. It was a sad day and I played the tape back of all what she had done for me. My kids cried as well. I asked for certain things which we got when we married and was denied by the sisters and son. All my belongings in storage was never returned to me. What she could salvage upon the foreclosure was forever gone. I knew they blamed me for her death which was foolish and unreasonable, but when death happens families draw their lines in the sand.

My Nur

I have been devastated, overwhelmed, and shattered by many things in my life yet today I once again am confronted with loss. We all have those who are a part of our lives who regardless of the ups and downs, we love. Even when separation may have become an outcome we never forsake those moments when someone really cared and we knew we were loved. Today it is a celebration in some respect because my former wife is no longer physically suffering. I say ex-wife but in reality we were never truly departed from one another. I still confided in her and always did what I could to help her. She took an inexperienced young man and breathed life into me. She shaped and placed my feet on the firmness of life. She decorated me with a substance that was rich and courageous. I will never forget her nor shall my children ever forget those times when she gave them a chance at life to be human beings of value. It is strange today knowing she is gone physically and that her spirit is alive, rejoicing in an everlasting sanctuary of love and peace.

To her I salute and honor the very life she lived and gave to me. I will cry tears of pain because that is what loss does at times to us, and I will become sadden just for today and at moments when I can feel her still shrouding my nature with an indescribable love and care, I will smile. So yes it hurts, yet my love for her will always be chronicled on the banks of joy. I ask her to forgive me for all I did that may have disturbed her heart or caused a discomfort. Just for today she has the victory because death is a conquest, it is a moment that we surrender our reasons to live yet win because we no longer have to fight life. We yield and in relinquishing our lives it is a triumph to return to our creator. It is a moment to unite back from which we come. Farewell and peace to you Nur Amin; someone remarkable and someone I will always keep close; even death cannot partition what I feel for you, nor will there ever be a day that passes that your magnificence will not be felt. I let you go now....soar towards an endless light of peace, tranquility, and calm. I am a man in pain.

CHAPTER 7
THE HOME STRETCH

Spiritualism

I have always been interested in the differences life presents. My life was coming along and I was dealing with me. I was a single parent and working each and every day. I stopped going to masjid and basically stopped practicing on a daily basis. I just felt empty listening to rules and policies. I wanted to seek out for myself what could feed me the purpose of who I am. I am not what I thought I was, nor did I believe this was all there was. I wanted more of why, and the search for why became a quest. I still was taking an online course and listening to Deepak Chopra and a host of other visionaries. I purchased a book on Buddhism and researched meditation. I found out that there is an energy that transcends all boundaries and we all are a part of the source. I then began to order books on different information and I really became inspired by Tony Robbins, Les Brown and the world renowned Jim Rohn. Then there was the master himself, Dr. Wayne Dwyer. These characters and a host of other people pointed me somewhere where I started to digest and consume something more than rhetorical speeches. I had been halfway around the world looking for me and what is my purpose.

It all began by running off with the circus of pain. There were those who thought I would be better off with a suit of pain. I took what they fitted me in and forfeited 25-years of my life participating in my own destruction. I was homeless, mainlining heroin, cocaine and peddling me in every way that could have killed me. I wanted love in all the wrong places and from all the wrong people. I looked for God in so many things which I thought would get me acceptance and love. The years came with me always banged-up; and He decided He would spare me. I have committed many crimes against myself and to others. If I got what I truly deserved, I would have been out of here long ago. I was a vagabond and derelict; someone who in his running away did so much harm. Forgiving oneself is not as easy as one may think.

This is why it became a fulfillment to see the clues along the road of my journey pointing me towards me. I could feel me for the first time, and at times a total stranger would take up a conversation with me, pointing me onward. I started listening to Ms. Oprah Winfrey and her *Super Soul Sunday* show. The guests she had seemed as though they were talking directly to me. I ordered each book from most of the guests she had on that show. I would take notes and it appeared they were all saying the same thing but differently. The list of people were absolutely enlightening and even Ms. Oprah Winfrey herself became a teacher; each show helping me to find me. I would run into total strangers and it would be like they were sent to me to discuss the divine within me.

This new meal of understanding for me was an area I had longed for. It was accepting me and not following any particular policy or rules and regulations. I started to uncover what had been missing all my life. I looked at things as I am a part of an energy source. Something as dipping a cup into the ocean and you have a cup of the ocean in your grasp; I am a part of this massive source of love. It is all about love. Love is the answer to so many issues. The list of books I started to examine and come to be grateful for was Miguel Ruiz' *The Four Agreements,* where he talks about living through four agreements; making your word impeccable; truthful without lacing it with sin.

All my life I spewed poison upon myself and others. I lied and wished harm on others because it is easier to point at those outside of me for faults or because they told me the truth. Some tried to love me and I had so much sin and anger that I refused to be loved. Then it was personalizing every little thing that happened in my life. My marriages failed and I was a failure because of me taking things personal. Mr. Ruiz also mentions making assumptions in life which I lived by. I assumed so many things were one way when in reality it was far from reality and the truth. Then it was never becoming the best I could be. I was always settling for lower-than-life things. I never wanted to be what I was destined to be. Greatness scared me! I was refusing to become that monumental person I was supposed to be. This has always been an issue of me dishonoring me, for the sake and welfare of others. This became evident from early on how I would ensure *'you are okay'* and that *'your life or situation is doing well,'* while I am in despair or just making it. This newfound spiritual lift is not for everyone and many have different ways of ascending. Religion was a small aspect of my life, where I trusted the religion's ways and means to bring me some sort of redemption and keep me on the straight path. With my spiritual fulfillment I had a chance to grow personally inside. I could have private sessions with the source, God. I could soar without restrictions or going to check whether this was appropriate or not.

There was other literature I explored that raised the level of my consciousness in some respect. I was able to move beyond the usual and trust in love and the universe. It is not easy and most will think you are on something or not understand your thought process. I recall telling someone about the chattering and roommate in my head (EGO) and they suggested I go talk to someone – not knowing we all have this trying to mislead our hearts. This newfound relief has always been there, whispering to me, and trying to keep me aligned whereas I was not ready because of the concealment of the divine I possess.

I read once where showing my embarrassments, my flaws, the instabilities I possess, are nothing to be ashamed of, it makes me or anyone fearless. Unclothing me and just be me, not wearing the mask of what others want me to display. The spiritual path I have finally discovered also made me less fearful of death, and I welcome whatever the universe rolls out for me. It is all in the design. I have the source of my beginnings and my end. It is amazing all the regions and landscapes I traveled along looking for acceptance, love to be a part of was within. I changed my name thinking I needed to be that name, not knowing it is not in the name, but what daily actions I take to be genuine and kind. I started meditating to quiet the chattering and to listen to my spirit. Prayer is something we do outwardly and meditating is quieting ourselves to let God speak to us.

Acceptance

How exciting it was to discover me! How marvelous it was to strip me and see that what I had looked all over for was within me! It bewildered me to finally say that. It was beyond mere conception and as I internalized this phrase of divine meanings, implications, and references I unraveled me more. I started to walk easier and see more clearly. There are still life's challenges, bills, debts, emotional sagas, but I am better today in dealing with the finality of an amazing life. The years I ran away to parts unknown with a suit a pain, acceptance and forgiveness was my antidote. I have accepted me for whom I am. I was just speaking to someone before writing this finality of a wonderful life I lived. I have no regrets for living the life I did, for it was given to me – to live with the choices I made. I forgive me for the abstract way in which I lived, the arenas, the broken hearts, the failures I constructed, and all that which kept me out of the alignment of being I that I am.

The biggest issues we face sometimes in life is acceptance. Accepting the things we have no control over and the things we cannot change. As bad as our instincts desire to capture the moment and possess it, we can only get out of the way and understand we cannot be the main attraction as bad as we long for. Bit players; those who join in supporting roles truly are those confidants who although their role is minimal seem to steal the show at times. Even if they do not, they still are self-fulfilled inside knowing they played a part.

My trouble was always thinking it was all about me. Coming to terms in any situation is growth and when we can remove our selfishness and bias we can develop into refined works of art. Human masterpieces! I have no doubt that God uses those as He sees fit. He brings forth those in our lives for seasons and in those seasons of uncertainty we must surrender to what we will never be able to control. And within the margin of error, there will be the stigma of sufficiency that has allowed one to check themselves for the variances that not accepting can cause.

How befuddling control is as thought and acted upon. How delusional this attribute of compulsion was for me. The obsession it caused and how if not careful, can sidetrack anyone. So just for today the lesson is acceptance. Accepting those circumstances we cannot change, those set of principals which are not meant for us to change, those matters where we are only spectators who for the grace of God played a part in changing someone else's life or thoughts especially mine; that is the blessing. Learning to accept and not look past the difference you have made in others' lives. We can only govern our own affairs and thank God, the Divine Spirit for being able to accept His decree and get out of the way before we trip into an intersection of difficulty as I did for so many years. I accept what was and receive what is yet to come.

I welcome the universe to continue to unfold wonders for me, allow me to soar beyond the ordinary, and let me touch upon the many surprises life offers and shows. All that has taken a segment in time. All those people who came and went through my life were part of the story, my abusers, victims, and those just stopping through to write about in my book of my life; and that is what it is – life showcases events, responses and outcomes as the motivational speaker and Author John Maxwell eloquently put it. How we react to the events is the telling of the outcome we will receive. The events that happened, I gave a conditional response over and over again and this is why my outcome was always sending me back to the same event over and over again. It is said making the same mistake over and over again is the most accurate evidence of insanity.

Who would ever think a kid born in New York and raised in the Valley of the Township of Orange would become what I have become. I am alive! Those who wrote me off, barred me, and did their best to wrong me, I forgive. I wore a cloak of disappointment and pain and I only invited times that I wanted to happen. Sometimes in life, as Dr. Judith Orloff states in her book *'Surrender,'* which is about suffering and abusers; that abusers know sufferers and they place them in one another's grasp. In other words, my many trips down the road of life, I was distinct as seeking one to abuse me playing the role as the sufferer and me seeking the sufferer out to abuse, a cycle of pain nevertheless. Love as I mentioned is the only option for me. I am thankful for living through what I went through and there are those out there who experienced much worse and never got a chance to share their story. I needed to tell about me, and it is okay because what I discovered is I am a human being and not an animal, and we all ask God for things in life. I asked for courage and God did not give me courage. He gave me an opportunity to practice being courageous by letting you see me not spotless.

Harvest for Healing

In life we are faced with situations we are not in control of. Some individuals cannot come to terms with the trauma that changed their course of reason, leaving a mark, indentation, scarring their existence, where living through pain is a daily occurrence. How do we first bandage our lives, and then remove the bandages and begin to live? There will always be painful events that come into our lives, yet some of us have a difficult time moving forward. There is a scab that we pick at and we never give ourselves a chance to heal.

Our life becomes unwilling, reluctant, and unenthusiastic. We align ourselves to things which temporary relieves the suffering we take ourselves through. We act-out in all kinds of manners, causing more harm and alienating us from society. Our attitudes become undisciplined and badly behaved. Our alignment to be centered is off because trauma has ravished our nature. Our pain spills over to our communities contributing to decay, mold, rotting the hearts and souls of the inhabitants. Wronged individuals emotionally injured, causing their choices and direction to be ill equipped. There are multitudes that are fastened to an ideology induced by pain; suffering, willingly becoming damaged goods. The process for healing is detaching oneself from that part of us that needs to be discarded and disposed.

Many have no idea how to change from their wounded existence. It is imperative an exodus is needed along with disentangling from negatives, initiating forgiveness, and exonerating oneself from the obscurity and shame we have lived with. Do away with the sorrows. Those are the guilt mechanisms we shield under. There is a gathering of our shattered souls convening for moments in time, to unravel ask for forgiveness through the harvest for healing.

Love

I have never had me where I could truly be affectionate with me, to breathe on me. I am in love with me although there has been loss and gains; I said this to someone about the years I have lost never to be recaptured or relived. He told me in those years in obscurity presented who I am today. Look at all I accomplished and what it produced. It shows how periodically, I still may not realize the greatness in me. I was told my determination and infatuation with women was my inability to just be me. I would rather dishonor me, possibly making-up to women, for the abuse I did to my mother; I have no idea, all things are possible. I know that I love beauty in everything and there is someone we all have an inclination towards, but I have no idea where it will go. It is that young lady who I wrote about early on that was younger and audacious, bold and inviting. Even though after years of winking at one another we decided to have a cup of tea, it was glorious and she breathed on me. I always looked for her in my life to be breathed upon; someone who I could become emotionally uncovered with that I did not have to hold back my story. I have told her my story and I love the fact I can feel her as she feels me.

I have no idea what tomorrow will bring. I was a kid ripped apart by those who thought it would be exciting to see the terror on my face. Through their actions and abuse, I held that scream for so long, and I gave others the terror they gave me, by disrespecting my mother, bringing hardship in my relationship's and just being an animal. I left my markings along the corridor of disappointment and it took breaking me down, to find a light on that mountain. Yes, I abused me more than anyone. I suffered because this is what I thought I should do. I blame no one for my actions or thoughts during those times. It took so many years of painful living, yet I see what I have become today. I am wealthy within. I will not allow anyone to tell me I cannot. It took so long to write this, wanting the world to take a look at me, and hopefully, the love I am sharing will help someone. It is about healing. I asked so many people who I may have hurt to forgive me and to allow me to make a completion with them. So many I have wronged and I wrote to them letters of completion declaring what I felt and to put an end to whatever was still out there. I have decency within my soul and everything I too ran away from, I accept as just me.

The Search for Me

The search for me has been long and challenging. It has been a journey through murkiness and moments where darkness was my home. The search for me was in relationships, new demographics, religions, new clothes, and just about anything I thought would help to define me. What is my purpose? What was the meaning of me? I decided to run away with the circus because they said I was a clown and I believed I was an amusement of some sort of character of loathe.

The search for me involved inflicting pain and suffering along the road, because that is what I thought I was supposed to do. The search for me, had I hospitalized my face needing plastic surgery after someone thought my face was good for his bat. I crawled out of an alley with a wound; they did not know what it was – a gun shot, a knife – who knows, maybe a rat.

The search for me found me...along the Hudson River painting rocks with arts and crafts as a daily thing for people like me who still have not found themselves. Then one day I went to a mountain...an odd looking mountain where there was a burning bush and I threw up all the pain from not knowing me. I ran away and was now found. I lost and gained 25 years with the circus and when I found me, I was right – here all the time. I just thought I needed everything in the world to make me. I will die and I thank God, although I may have a hole in my boat, I found me. I am coming home. The search for me is over. I found Earl in the light and what an amazing person I am...It has been a journey and let it be thought about when my eyes do finally close... I was me and loved.

The Lord Had Spoken and Touched Me

All my life I was a prisoner of my own madness and insecurities. It all began on a day when I saw no more sunshine, pain welcomed me and shame straddled me in for a ride of guilt and sadness. Clouds and storms of discontent introduced itself as part of my anguish for I was devastated and tarnished with exploitation. You see, on that day I turned away from God and welcomed degradation and hardship as a coat for me to adorn. I struggled through the murkiness and quandary of ignorance. I sat in self-pity as my life headed towards a pit of iniquity.

The time I spent wandering through life, with this cloak upon my shoulders, the many times I have tried to remove it yet it was stitched to me. I lay in the gutter of life…not knowing my Lord, did not have a clue I was self-destructing. My loved ones cried and my mother prayed, cried tears of forgiveness for me beseeching the Lord to cover and protect me. My broken spirit scattered across the landscape of life, I needed something to release my pain.

Then on a day I least expected I began to climb out of that gutter, angels of mercy beckoned me and I screamed out, shedding the suit and cloak of pain which held me a prisoner. My life story is not unique nor is it one you have not heard of before. I was traumatized, shaken into a mold of shame, guilt, and hopelessness. After my release I trembled in joy for the world was different from what I was accustomed to. Someone smiled at me, someone said hello and then the sun began to shade my existence and I cried. I cried because I thought He had forgotten me. I thought I was worthless, unloved, a misfortune of life. I was given a divine brush of forgiveness and I scrubbed myself cleaning, renewing myself in his name. The Lord had spoken and touched me.

In Conclusion

ME

Nothing is more precious than life itself and although the pains of living are attached to me, I live onward embracing the embarrassments and flaws I possess. And in exposing and fastening these discomfiture's to my existence, the tenderness of opening my heart to show me makes me fearless. I am a better me, by perishing that part of me which need not be attached anymore. I am recreated, renewed and resurrected to a pristine me.

I AM THAT I AM

IN MEMORIUM

Dear Muhammad Ali,

Until today, I never knew what your death would mean to me. I knew one day I would have to say farewell. Before the publication of my memories, I want to say to you how much of an impact you have had on my life. It was you who demonstrated the epitome of manhood by standing upon your convictions. It was always you who I looked to as an example of strength and respect. You have helped so many define the meaning of character with your integrity to stand-up for what you believe in. I saw a man with courage – a man with respectability... I saw a man with decency, love and integrity... I saw a man with morality. I heard a man say 'I Am The Greatest'... I saw Muhammad Ali.

January 17, 1942 – June 4, 2016

I would like to recognize the late Carl Sharif (Newark, New Jersey) for his courage, determination and love for making change. The late Reverend Dr. Ronald B. Christian, Pastor of Christian Love Baptist Church (Irvington, New Jersey) who forwarded a letter to former New Jersey Governor Jon A. Corzine, petitioning Executive Clemency (Pardon) on my behalf which was granted. These two giants I will keep close to my memories. Thank you to the many people and organizations which helped me to survive this thing we call life. I also want to acknowledge in some respect those who died in the lifestyle; succeeding in destroying themselves, something I failed at, or were victims of other behaviors detrimental to their wellbeing.

There are many more people who died too soon and too sudden. Some live and some died and I was given another chance to live. There are also to be recognized the many parents, especially the mothers and siblings, who endured years of worry and hardships. I know myself of what I put my mother through and there were many other mothers and fathers whose hearts were broken and went to graves as my moms did unknowing what would prevail in their child's life. My prayers are with all.

TESTIMONIALS

"Buck Naked by Earl Scott takes one on a roller coaster journey of life where the audience will come to know the struggles of self-discovery, the fear of greatness, and the power of love and forgiveness...a powerful read." – Marvin V. Curtis

"Very powerful book! When I read Buck Naked I found myself taking a deep breath and releasing it. I could relate to some of your story. Buck Naked held my attention from the beginning to end and there is so much in your story that will help someone out there that is going through similar situation or has experienced trauma and pain. Glory to God for uplifting and instilling integrity, honesty and dignity in the man behind the word." – Ann Brown

"Your book is a must read. I am pleased that I had to opportunity to experience your journey with you. I cried, I smiled, and I prayed sometimes all at once. I thank God for all that He is blessing you with. Praying that you will be successful beyond your dreams."
– Sakinah Sylvia Barnett

"I read your book with an objective eye and open heart, without judgment. Each chapter stirred my soul with a flood of heart-filled emotions. You see, your story is blemished with the pain and scars of shame so many in all communities have suffered, but was too shameful and scared to share. This book is about healing and should be read by mothers and fathers, so that their child, male or female will be protected from the monsters. What an act of bravery to unclothe yourself naked. I too felt buck naked."
– Amanda M. Koon

ABOUT THE AUTHOR

Education
Current – Ph.D. Candidate
Walden University
Public Health

2004 – Master Business of Administration
University of Phoenix
Specialization in Health Care Management

2002 – Bachelor of Science
DeVry University
Telecommunications Management

Coursera Online Certificates of Completion
Case Western Reserve University
Inspiring Leadership through Emotional Intelligence

University of Copenhagen
The New Nordic Diet - From Gastronomy to Health

Vanderbilt University
Nutrition, Health, and Lifestyle: Issues and Insights

University of Toronto
Social Concepts in Mental Health

University of Manchester
Global Health and Humanitarianism

Emory University
The Bible's Prehistory, Purpose, and Political Future

University of Pennsylvania
Growing Old around the Globe
Introduction to Key Concepts and Supreme Court Cases

University of Pennsylvania – Wharton
Better Leader, Richer Life

University of California (San Francisco)
Nutrition for Health Promotion and Disease Prevention

Stanford University
Child Nutrition and Cooking

University of Albany – Online
Preparedness & Community Response to Pandemics
Microbiology: An Introduction
Nuclear Terrorism: Pathways and Prevention
Terrorism, Preparedness, and Public Health Introduction
Orientation to Public Health
Health Literacy & Public Health Module I and II

Sudden Infant Death Syndrome and Post-Partum Depression

Case Studies
2007 – *Policy Change and Health Promotion Planning*
Community Health Worker
Hepatitis: (A) Outbreak

Honors and Awards
2016 – The Lifers Group – Department of Corrections

2015 – City of Newark Municipal Council, Newark, New Jersey – *RESOLUTION*

New Jersey Department of Corrections
Outstanding Volunteer Services Appreciation Award

2014 – New Jersey Department of Corrections
Inmate Mentoring

2013 – The Lifers Group – East Jersey State Prison
Contributions for Making a Difference

The Greater Conservancy of New Jersey
The Nelson Mandela Freedom Gardening Award

2012 – New York University Black Student Alliance
Public Service Award

Essex County Prosecutors Office of Victims' Witness Advocacy

The Associates in Mental Health and Developmental Disabilities
The President's Executive Leadership Award

Harvard School of Government
City of Newark Re-Entry Program

2011 – New Jersey Chapter of American Correctional Association
New Jersey Department of Labor and Workforce Development Award

New Jersey Department of Community Affairs and New Jersey State League of Municipalities
Recognition of Newark's Prisoner Re-Entry Initiatives

Edna Mahan Correctional Facility for Women
Certificate of Appreciation Recognition

2010 – The Prospect Employment Services
Certificate of Appreciation

The National League of Cities (Innovative Economic Development)
Innovation and Governance Award

Edna Mahan Correctional Facility for Women
Certificate of Appreciation Recognition

2008 – Superior Court of New Jersey – *Recognition*
City of Newark, New Jersey – *Recognition*

2006 – International Inter-Religious Community
Ambassador for Peace Award
State of New Jersey Department of Military and Veterans Affairs

2001 – Telecommunications Management Association
Certificate of Achievement

2004 – The American Legion – The Georgia Service Veteran – *Distinguished Service*

2003 – Clayton State University (Morrow, Georgia) Toast Masters Charter Member
Best Speaker Award

Society for Human Resources Management Certificate

1999 – Superior Court of New Jersey
Supervisory Award Recognition
Outstanding Performance Award

1998 – *Outstanding Leadership Award*

1996 – National Safety Council
New Jersey Islamic Schools
PTA President's Award Honoree

City of Newark
Employee of the Month

National Safety Council Certification

Letters of Recognition
1997 – 1998 – 2001 – 2002
The Honorable Mayor Sharpe James – City of Newark

2002 – City of Newark Municipal Council

2000 – City of Newark Municipal Council Members:
Councilwoman-at-Large Betsey Walker
Councilwoman Mamie Bridgeforth
State of New Jersey Senator Ronald Rice

Volunteer Services
Henry County Medical Center Auxiliary – Georgia
American Red Cross – 9/11/01
New Jersey Department of Corrections

Community Activities
1999-2000 Coalition of Religions
Promoting Public Health Initiatives HIV/AIDS

2000 – Bridging the Gap Organization – President
Promoting Quality of Life

Membership Affiliations
American Public Health Association (APHA)
American College of Health Executives (ACHE)
Honorably Discharged Veteran/Notary
Society for Human Resources Management
Telecommunications Management Association
<u>The Visions Metro</u> – Newark – Contributing Columnist